Bearing Witness

Churches Caring for Migrants and Refugees

Carol Brown

Doorlight Publications
Clinton, Massachusetts and Abington, Pennsylvania

ISBN 0-9982233-3-6
ISBN13 978-0-9982233-3-9

Cover image: Carol Brown
Cover and Interior Design: Ruth Anne Burke

To the refugees and migrants who have shared your stories with us. Your lives and faces are imprinted on my heart and mind.

To those who served faithfully on the Board of Directors and entrusted me with oversight of the program for seven plus years.

To the many volunteers, too numerous to count or name, who served alongside me and inspired me by your sacrificial love and care for the vulnerable.

To my family, and especially Dan, who walked alongside me, celebrating the joys and shouldering the struggles. You have listened, strategized, created, and served to keep the program open and to allow all of us to serve.

Thank you

Contents

Preface

This book is one small collection of stories of the women, children, and men served by a group of churches in downtown Istanbul. Together the churches have been caring for migrants and refugees for 34 years. Dozens, maybe even hundreds, of books could be written if the other coordinators or the many faithful volunteers were to share their memories and experiences. Thousands more volumes would be added if the refugees and migrants themselves were to tell their own stories.

These stories bear witness to the faithfulness of God. They offer only a glimpse of a remarkable work, and I write only from my limited perspective. This is not a history of the refugee program, though that book, were it possible to write, would also testify to the faithfulness of God. But I hope these stories will lead you to marvel at God and the work of his church, and that you will be moved to find ways to love and serve the vulnerable in your corner of the world.

This book also bears witness to the God who is with us. The story is a part of the bigger story of God, his work in the world, and his call on his people to bear witness to him. The presence of God in the garden office has made it a sacred space. In our current world of chaos, and as we witness cruelty meted out to strangers in our midst, these stories need to be heard. This is a call to the global church, to followers of Jesus everywhere, to see and serve refugees and migrants, widows and orphans, the hungry, the poor, and the prisoner in obedience to his command and in response to his love.

I am grateful to Matt and to Lynsey for their valuable feedback on the manuscript. My daughter, Ruth Anne, deserves thanks for shaping the manuscript into a book. Most of all, I am indebted to Dan for serving as my coach and editor. He knew there was a story to be shared. He never pushed me but was patient throughout the long process of recalling and recording these stories.

Prologue

The King will answer them, "Truly, I say to you, as you did it to one of the least of these my brothers, you did it to me."

Matthew 25:40

When I first entered the Church of the Resurrection in Anafora, Egypt, I was stunned; nothing prepared me for what I saw.

A ninety-minute drive north from Cairo on the Alexandria Road, the cathedral is nestled within the Anafora Coptic Orthodox community. It is more than nestled; it is almost submerged in the desert. A driveway of interlocking bricks and scattered potholes demands a slow approach. Drive too fast and you will likely miss it altogether. Bougainvillea hedgerows hide the domes and crosses unless you know to look. Arched domes rise only to ground level, and the clay exterior blends with the surrounding sand.

Follow a winding, walled pathway downward to the entrance, and suddenly sandy brown gives way to a vibrant cascade of color. The first image I saw was a panda. The exterior portrays scenes of the Old Testament: creation, fall, flood, covenant, exodus, exile, and prophets. Walk through the door, and the old covenant gives way to the new. Suddenly I was fully immersed in the stories of Jesus like never before. The whole space, floor to ceiling, is covered in vivid, vibrant icons of the birth, life, death, and resurrection of Jesus Christ. Meticulous detail transports you into the scenes. As a place of worship, the church is a rich display of the visual narrative of faith. The child in me was in awe at the larger-than-life colorful scenes. I wish this had been my growing-up experience rather than small, poster-size pictures of Jesus tacked to a cement wall.

We entered for our first visit without any expectations. Right away I was breathless and in awe. It was an experience like few others I have known. I have been in places where icons covered the walls, but those felt distant and grand. These images are close and intimate. Rag rugs cover the floors and the chairs. They add warmth, color, culture, and an invitation to sit down and spend time. I smiled as I looked up to see the same rag rugs in icons depicting heaven. The floor of heaven matched where I was standing. The air is cool even with the desert sun beating down, as the space is submerged in the earth. The colors – stunning! We gave each other space and time to just sit, to walk, to marvel at the experience.

Then I came to the icon representing Jesus at the end of the age, separating those who had truly known and followed him from those who said that they did. The passage from Matthew 25:35-40 has long been significant to me, and here were the words of Jesus vividly imagined: "For I was hungry and you gave me something to eat, I was thirsty and you gave me something to drink, I was a stranger and you invited me in, I needed clothes and you clothed me, I was sick and you looked after me, I was in prison and you came to visit me," Jesus said. But the righteous answered, "Lord, when did we see you hungry and feed you, or thirsty and give you something to drink? When did we see you a stranger and invite you in, or needing clothes and clothe you? When did we see you sick or in prison and go to visit you?" Jesus answered, "Truly I tell you, whatever you did for one of the least of these brothers and sisters of mine, you did for me."

In the icon, the King is Christ; the hungry one is Christ; the thirsty one is Christ; the stranger is Christ; the naked is Christ; the sick is Christ; the prisoner is Christ. The icon is a powerful visual reminder of our calling as followers of Jesus–to care for the hungry, the thirsty, the strangers in our midst, the naked, the sick, and those in prison. At all times, in every period of history, in every place, this call is the same. "The poor you will always have with you," Jesus told his disciples. What we offer to the least of these, we offer to him.

Eleven hundred kilometers north of this sacred space on the Alexandria Road is another sacred space. The walls there are not vibrant. The space is not grand. Nothing here would cause you to compare the two spaces–except this icon. One is a stunning cathedral; the other a tiny, one-room, garden office in downtown Istanbul. But in this space the Anafora icon has been lived out over the past 34 years as the churches of downtown Istanbul and their many volunteers have cared for refugees and migrants in the name of Jesus. This is a sacred space of a different kind. The vulnerable depicted in the Church of the Resurrection come to life in this small office as they share their stories and are met with compassion and grace. We shed tears together. We laugh together. We share comic foibles in translation. Yet in the laughter and the tears, love is the repeated theme and the driving motivation.

Hundreds of volunteers – some who served for one day and others for many years – form a fellowship that now spans the globe. For them the stories that I am sharing from my time of service are a sampling of what each of them carries with them from their time of serving. My prayer is that this collection of stories will stir each of us in our care for the strangers among us. I also pray that the book will evoke collective thanksgiving for the amazing work God has done and is doing through his people, the Church, to serve migrants and refugees in Istanbul.

The one-room office in the garden of the church in downtown Istanbul has witnessed many people come and go.

Over these 34 years, dozens of nations have been represented by hundreds of volunteers and visitors. The number of people cared for is well over ten thousand. No single set of stories can even begin to capture the experience of so many volunteers and visitors over such a length of time. The stories here are a small sampling of the stories of the children, women, and men we served and cared for. I was privileged to be a part of this extraordinary program over the past twelve years. I offer these memories with humble gratitude and ongoing amazement at what God has done. I entered this story when the center was already over twenty years old. Records bear witness to some of the past, and I can attest that God has been the one true constant. To God be the glory.

The stories that follow are the stories of real people, though I have changed the names.

Birth

So [Hagar] called the name of the LORD who spoke to her, "You are a God of seeing," for she said, "Truly here I have seen him who looks after me."

Genesis 16:13

For you formed my inward parts; you knitted me together in my mother's womb. I praise you, for I am fearfully and wonderfully made.

Psalm 139:13–14

Joan was young, scared, pregnant, a Congolese woman, alone and vulnerable in Istanbul. She spoke only French. Joan came to our gate at the urging of a coworker at the textile factory where she labored long hours each day. As she sat across from me, I saw her distress. Her eyes stared down at the floor, her shoulders rounded, leaning over her pregnant belly. Her hands fidgeted with the drawstring on her bag. Joan's baby had stopped moving. The baby had only just begun to be noticeably active over the past few weeks. Joan had delighted in feeling the kicks, even as she lay on her bed tired after work. Yesterday she had felt nothing. Last night the same. Joan could sense Gaspard's warm compassionate spirit as he translated her French. Joan's tears streamed down her cheeks. She feared that the baby was dead.

We gave Joan orange juice and asked her to sit quietly in the garden. Maybe the sugar would stir the baby to movement. She seemed to have no other health problems that might put her pregnancy at risk. No high blood pressure. No bleeding. "If only we had a Doppler," I thought to myself. A Doppler would allow us to listen for the baby's heartbeat. But there was no Doppler, and the orange juice made no difference. We sent Joan down to our nearby partner hospital to be examined. "Can I pray with you?" I asked Joan before she left. "Yes!" she eagerly replied. Together we entrusted her and her unborn child to the One who had made them and knew them intimately.

Joan returned with one of our volunteers, her newfound young American friend. Joan spoke no English; her companion spoke no French. But both were beaming. They did not need a common language to share the joy. They had both heard the baby's heartbeat.

Joan gave birth to a beautiful baby girl a few months later. Then, in the baby's early months, Joan with her precious bundle returned to her mother and extended family in Congo.

My vivid memory of that early encounter evokes the joy, wonder and relief that I and others on our team would feel over and over again when we heard the miracle of the beating heart of an unborn baby. Joan also left behind a practical legacy; she motivated us to purchase a doppler.

That was July 2014. Joan was one of the first women I served at our small refugee center. I had met Sue, the coordinator of the program, just a week earlier. "You are a nurse?" she asked me in surprise. "We need you! When can you start?" With excitement she invited me to join the team the following week. That was the start of more than a decade of caring for refugees and migrants in Istanbul, first as a volunteer, then as coordinator of this remarkable organization.

When I arrived that summer of 2014, the program had welcomed women like Joan for 22 years. Twelve years later, it continues into its fourth decade. Volunteers have cared for hundreds of vulnerable migrants and refugees each year. Yet a visitor to our tiny, nondescript office in the narrow church garden might never guess the significance or impact of what it represents. Those who launched the program could hardly have imagined the legacy they would leave.

The idea for a joint program to care for refugees and migrants was conceived in 1991, when church leaders in central Istanbul met together to share their concern over the common challenge they were facing. A fresh wave of migrants had come to Istanbul. Those who gathered knew that they were called to serve the vulnerable and displaced. Istanbul, where Asia and Europe meet, had been a crossroads for refugees and migrants for decades, indeed centuries. Members of each church had been doing what they could. Each church was acting alone, independent of one another, and they knew that it was not enough. People from all over Asia and Africa were making their way to Europe in search of a new start, a safe refuge, asylum from persecution, only to find themselves stranded in Turkey. Migrants were a constant, but in 1991 Istanbul, an expanding city of nine million people, was the landing place for a new wave of refugees fleeing war in Iraq. The need for aid, counsel and assistance had increased, but services available to migrants were minimal. The dozens of government and non-governmental organizations that now serve refugees were non-existent then. Church leaders were feeling the strain.

A proposal drafted at a meeting of Istanbul church leaders in March 1992 summarized the challenges they saw. Migrants, the Istanbul church leaders wrote, were battered by forces beyond their control, and cast "adrift from their home societies." After entering Turkey, they were granted "little sympathy from Turkish officialdom" and little access to assistance. They hoped to move on, but "the doors for further migration from Turkey are, in the main, legally closed." Consequently, "illegal means of migration" were a thriving industry. The description of the challenges facing migrants in this early proposal remains eerily applicable more than 30 years later.

In this situation, the proposal insists, the responsibility of Christians was inescapable. Churches are obliged, "by their own internal theological and moral mandate," to fill the gap and to take the challenge seriously. Those who met together saw the challenge of caring for migrants as primarily a pastoral problem and a collective obligation. Individual efforts and informal coordination were insufficient for the task. The churches needed to work together, "to shoulder this immense and multifaceted pastoral task more deliberately and effectively." 34 years later the challenges faced by migrants are the same and the mandate of the church is unchanged.

When Bob and Olga, the first coordinators, welcomed vulnerable migrants and refugees in October of 1992, they were acting out the vision expressed by church leaders. They were being the continued presence of Jesus to the vulnerable. They were also seeing the presence of Jesus in the vulnerable; living out the words of Christ in Matthew 25:40, "Truly, I say to you, as you did it to one of the least of these my brothers, you did it to me."

Many things have changed over the decades – volunteers, coordinators, programs, conflict zones from which refugees flee, the legal environment, technology, partner organizations and the migrants and refugees themselves. But the foundations of our calling have remained constant. Amidst a changing world we have continued to focus on the most vulnerable, offer hospitality, listen with respect and compassion, counsel wisely, assess and treat what we can, refer to other partner organizations, connect to community and resources. Some of those coming to us have had little education and the majority are removed from their families and traditional sources of intergenerational wisdom and experience. They are vulnerable. Part of the challenge and joy of this work has been adapting to the needs of those in our care, adjusting to the changing climate towards refugees, and accommodating to changes in the larger world of NGOs.

Fatma came to us that same summer of 2014, pregnant with her sixth child. When Fatma sat down, tears filled her eyes. "Could you please help me get rid of the baby?" she pleaded. Life was too hard. The family was stressed. Fatma's husband grew angry when he learned that she was pregnant. He had hit her, hoping that she would lose the child. This was too much to bear. Fatma and I cried together. I tried to encourage her. Despite the struggles and stresses, this new unborn life was precious, formed by God. We sent Fatma for a prenatal check at Saint George, our partner hospital, and gave her food coupons. She returned to us every month. We assured her that we would help with birth costs. Volunteers played with her children and did creative crafts with them. Fatma received clothing, rent money, hot meals, and compassionate care. She told us on several visits that our care was different than anything she had experienced before. Over time her smile grew, and her face brightened. She came to accept her growing belly, and she reported that she removed herself from situations that felt like they could become violent. Her children were safe, she reassured us.

In her eighth month of pregnancy, Fatma's oldest son, hoping to eventually reach Germany, hired smugglers to take him by boat to Europe. Fatma's heart was deeply saddened, but she hoped this would open a future in Europe for all of them. Then, a few weeks later, Fatma arrived at the center beaming. She had a baby boy! Having a boy is considered a special blessing, and Fatma humbly realized that she had wanted to abort this child. Because of this, she was all the more overwhelmed at the gift of a son. Her heart softened to hearing of God's love for her.

The next summer, in 2015, she suddenly stopped coming to any programs. She was never at the gate. We could only wonder if she and her five children had left Turkey. No goodbyes. No answers. That was the summer when a massive wave of migrants formed across Asia, the Middle East, and Africa, and flooded into Europe.

"You are made in the image of God." "You are beautiful." "You have value." These phrases were ones that I found myself repeating often. Women needed to be affirmed. Many women who come to us carry hidden burdens far heavier than just their difficult circumstances.

Aisha, a beautiful, thirty-two-year-old Afghan woman sat across from me holding a precious newborn girl. She had come to show receipts from her birth costs and to be reimbursed. We oohed and aahed over her adorable daughter. But Aisha's eyes filled with tears. "What is wrong?" I asked. Her mother-in-law refused to speak to her, she said. She had given birth to a third girl. Until she produced a male child, she would be considered useless as a woman. Her beautiful newborn daughter added no value to the family. Tears came to my eyes too. This was far too heavy a burden for any woman to carry. While comforting her and cuddling the baby, I was also aware of a boiling passion in me at the cruelty of it all. This is not right! This is ignorance! I wanted to explain that the husband is responsible for the sex of the child!

But this was no time for passion or for justice. Aisha needed gentle, maternal love. I moved from behind my desk, and I put my arm around her. "You are beautiful," I told her. I told her that her eyes are deep and gorgeous. I told her that God made her with care and knew about her from the time she was in her mother's womb. I looked with Aisha at her perfectly formed daughter, and I pointed out the beauty before us. I asked Aisha to promise me that in the future, when her daughter gives birth to a girl, that she will celebrate! I shared that every child is precious in God's sight and made in the image of God. Aisha would go home to her mother-in-law, but I prayed that the love, care and affirmation had touched a chord deep within her and would last.

In such circumstances I often share that God is familiar with the details of our lives. God sees us. God knows us. He is not distant and uncaring. He knows our comings and our goings. The God who sees us wants us to see him and to know him. He wanted us to know him so much that he himself came in human form, Jesus, God's son, to walk and talk and live among us in recordable history. The God who created time and space took on human form so that we could know him and so that he could do for us what we could not do for ourselves, save us; rescue us. He came to redeem us. "Jesus, Emmanuel, the God who came to be with us," I prayed, "take seeds that are sown and awaken her heart to you!"

Labor and delivery nursing was not new to me. Before I began volunteering in Istanbul, I have been involved in maternal-child health care inside the Arctic Circle of Canada, the southern desert of Pakistan, the mega-city of Cairo, the inner city of Chicago, and now the heart of Istanbul. In rural hospitals and in high-risk labor and delivery units, I have seen the vulnerability of women as they enter a new, uncharted season of life. Mothers-to-be share the joy, the anxiety, the fear, and the hope, whether they give birth at home or in a hospital, whether they have no prenatal care or a well-supported pregnancy, whether they are teenagers or women in their 40s.

The evening I attended my first birth, during nursing training, I was disappointed, even irritated; rather than observing a C-section, I was assigned to give an enema to a woman in early labor. My supervisor thought that it was a priority for me to accomplish this basic skill. I stayed in the bathroom with the sixteen-year-old mother-to-be. She was fearful and alone. We had been together in the small bathroom for what felt like a very long time. I was impatient. She should finish, I tried to convince her, and then we could walk through a few more contractions. Suddenly, I realized she was pushing. This was not just normal pushing. Her face turned red, and she was groaning. I pulled the emergency cord for assistance. On the next push, I caught the baby in a towel before it landed in the toilet. My supervisor gave me an "A" for enemas. In the birth record, the presentation was listed as a "spontaneous splash." My career in maternal-child nursing was initiated in memorable fashion. My classmates, who had seen very little of the C-section from the back of the operating theater, were rather jealous at the end of that shift.

Many circumstances surrounding birth are out of a woman's control; birth is miraculous, awe-inspiring, and unpredictable. I first gave birth in a Chicago teaching hospital's high-risk labor and delivery unit, then in a rural mission hospital in Pakistan, and finally as a visitor to a small hospital in Rochester, New York, where I arrived nine months pregnant, having recently returned from living in Egypt. The settings may change, but the miracle does not. Nor do the challenges.

Birth can be fear inducing, and it is always life changing. Whether an unanticipated first child to a single parent or a sixth child to a loving family, change follows as part of the experience. If you add to these factors the weight of being displaced as a refugee, the challenges can seem overwhelming.

God's heart is moved with the needs of the vulnerable, and there are few who are more vulnerable than women who face the challenge of another life to care for. Because of these realities, the refugee center has prioritized care for pregnant women and newborn babies. We are not set up to deliver babies, though on occasion it has seemed that a birth could happen in our small office when a woman did not heed our advice to go to the hospital. Our job has been to urge women to find resources in their local area of this megacity. We encourage them to come back to us with receipts for reimbursement and to bring any test results for us to review. We provide prenatal vitamins throughout their pregnancy and while they are breastfeeding.

We have many rewarding, one-on-one teaching opportunities. Though Turkey has good and even advanced medical care, it is not always available to the displaced. We seek to serve in that gap. Most outcomes are miraculous and beautiful. But we have no control over a woman's experience, and our hearts can be broken when we hear that a woman in labor has been turned away from a hospital because of not having money, or when a woman is charged double the price because she lacks official documentation of personhood. Refugees very rarely have any records of personal medical history. Not knowing a woman's obstetrical history means that a doctor will more quickly opt for a Caesarean birth if any problems arise. Caesareans are inherently a greater risk for the mother and the baby, but they are lifesaving when necessary. Turkey has a concerningly high rate of Caesarean births, according to the World Health Organization. This fact increases the likelihood of a pregnant refugee woman with no prenatal care or medical history to have to undergo a Caesarean birth.

Much effort has been made globally over the past decades to increase the health of pregnant women and provide for better outcomes for newborns. Education and monitoring are part of reducing both the mortality rates of women and children at birth. But refugees and migrants are often excluded from these resources and programs.

For nine long years, Awa's husband was in Istanbul, sending money home to Awa and her son. They saw him on only two occasions in those years when he returned for business and to renew a passport. Awa's husband had often asked her to join him. Finally, he convinced her. She left their nine-year-old son in the care of his grandmother and came to Istanbul. Their son was now in school, and that opportunity would not be open to him in Istanbul.

To a newcomer like Awa, Istanbul can be overwhelming and intimidating. Like many economic migrants, she and her husband came to Istanbul hoping for opportunity. They did not hesitate to endure long separations from family and spouse if they imagined that it would lead to a better future for them or their children. But the challenges could be overwhelming. Awa's husband knew Turkish and was busy with his work. But Awa was floundering. Then she became pregnant. Many years had passed since her previous pregnancy. Awa was apprehensive. A friend referred her to our center, and we enrolled her in our prenatal program. We sent her for a doctor's appointment, an ultrasound, and bloodwork.

I vividly remember the day that I opened Awa's bloodwork results. Our translator brought a stack of envelopes from the hospital with results from women who had recently had bloodwork drawn. I opened them, one by one, recorded the results in our database, indicated that there was bloodwork to be picked up, and noted if any follow-up treatment was needed. When I opened Awa's results, I was heartbroken. She was HIV positive.

We called her in; we needed to talk about the implications for her care, a plan for the delivery, and post-birth care of the baby. Breastfeeding would be impossible. "It must be a mistake!" she cried. We could repeat the test, I told her, but it would make the best sense for both Awa and her husband to go for bloodwork.

Awa came back in tears the following week. Her husband refused to be tested. He denied any other sexual relations. Slowly over some weeks, his denial and defensiveness wore down as Awa grieved and continued to probe and talk about what would need to be done. Awa was devastated to learn that her husband had in fact had multiple sexual partners, both male and female, over the years of their separation. She was heartbroken, betrayed, alone, and angry. As she pressed her husband on the consequences if he did not seek treatment, he finally agreed to be tested. Our volunteers supported both of them and treated them with care and respect. We gave Awa the opportunity to share her fears and express the gaps in her own understanding of what this would mean.

Awa delivered a beautiful baby girl. Some months after the birth the small family of three chose to repatriate to their home country where treatment for HIV was readily available. They left committed to one another as they faced the unknowns ahead.

Birth comes with a backstory as we see in the experiences of Joan, Fatma, Aisha and Awa. The joy of a new life is often mingled with pain.

This was true for Hagar, the young Egyptian slave of Sarai, the wife of Abram, in Genesis 16. Hagar had a backstory. Hagar was an alien. She was a foreigner in Canaan and in the household of Abram and Sarai she was a slave. Sarai gave her to Abram to provide an offspring on Sarai's behalf. But after she conceived, relations with Sarai got tense. Sarai, who had herself dreamed up this solution to produce an heir, went to Abram to complain. He told Sarai to do as she pleased. "Solve it yourself," he seemed to say. And Sarai did. She dealt harshly with Hagar, who fled into the desert.

God found Hagar in the wilderness. He saw her in her distress, and he promised her that her son would have a future. He would not be a servant of anyone. He would face trouble. He would live apart from others around him. But he would have a future. At the command of the angel of God, Hagar returned, though vulnerable, to the shelter of the household, reassured that God saw her and listened to her: "Truly I have seen him who looks after me." Often I shared Hagar's story with women who came to us, burdened by their pregnancy and hopeless with life circumstances, to remind them that God sees them, that God cares for them, that they have value.

In the garden office of our small refugee center, births were often followed by absences. Some mothers moved on to new countries, either being resettled officially, repatriating home, or possibly risking moving on with smugglers. Others disappeared from our program into the city's vastness and may reappear years later with a new crisis. Their stories remind us that every beginning is shadowed by uncertainty. For those women who remained in Istanbul– widows, single mothers, the displaced, and the undocumented, with whom we still had contact – we saw that loneliness becomes its own burden. The next chapter turns to these women and to the God who remains their protector.

Alone

Father of the fatherless and protector of widows is God in his holy habitation.

Psalm 68:5

The Lord watches over the sojourners; he upholds the widow and the fatherless.

Psalm 146:9

"Is there anything you can do to help me?" the young Afghan woman pleaded, as she held her two-year-old daughter Sarah while her four-year-old son Yusuf played on the playground at the back of the garden. Hanife had already endured more trauma than any woman should have to face. To be young, Afghan, and female was challenge enough. But she was also a refugee, displaced, separated from family, and undocumented.

In early spring 2021, Hanife and her husband, Mohammad, paid smugglers to transport them to Turkey. Hanife was pregnant. During the month-long journey, her passport was lost. She did not know how. Was it stolen by the smugglers? While traveling through Iran, Hanife gave birth to her firstborn, Yusuf. On arrival in Turkey, Mohammad was taken into detention. Miraculously, he was released, but he lived in fear that he would be detained by the police and deported. He became determined to move on from Turkey to find refuge. Because he had worked for the German government in Afghanistan, return to Afghanistan was not an option.

After Hanife learned she was pregnant with her second child, she heard of our program from a friend. Hanife asked us to assist her in arranging an abortion. She wanted our financial help. She told us of her husband's plan to leave Turkey for Europe. Her pregnancy was an obstacle to their plans. Yusuf would be burden enough on the difficult journey. They would need to carry him, and he would need to be kept quiet to escape attention.

We explained to Hanife that we could not help with an abortion, but that we could help with the cost of prenatal care and delivery. Meanwhile, Mohammad, fearful and anxious, decided to go ahead of the family to Germany. He didn't have enough money to pay a smuggler, and he feared the risky boat crossing, so he chose instead to rely on his phone's GPS to cross the border into Greece on foot. Once across, he would continue on to Germany.

Hanife was left alone in Istanbul, pregnant and caring for their toddler. How could she make life work here? Her story is repeated many times. Displaced Afghans often support each other. Sometimes neighbors take in a single mother and extend their already meager resources to care for her. But it is not always easy for either party and does not often last long. Hanife gave birth to her daughter Sarah alone in Istanbul.

Mohammad's sister and brother-in-law came from Afghanistan and lived with Hanife for a short time, but they too wanted to move on. They convinced her to attempt a boat crossing to Greece during the summer. They set off together, but they were separated into different boats. The boat that Hanife, Yusuf, and Sarah were in was intercepted by the Greek Coast Guard and returned to Turkey. They spent three months in detention in Izmir. When they were released, they were given permission to stay in Adana. Hanife knew no one in Adana, so she made her way back to Istanbul from Izmir without ever going south.

Hanife had legal permission to stay in Turkey for only one more month. Then what? She came to us asking, "Is there anything you can do?" Given the weight of her need, it feels inadequate to give her food coupons, a return appointment, and pray with her. We were also able to offer her a referral to the Moms and Tots program where volunteers could arrange for a visit to her home. For now, Hanife is here in

Istanbul hoping against hope that she and Mohammad will be reunited. Mohammad is waiting for his asylum case in Germany to be reviewed. He wants to be reunited with Hanife and the children, Yusuf and Sarah, but he can do little to help while he waits.

Circumstances like Hanife's often confronted us with our limitations. There is little we can do to sustain refugees in their situations. They have made many decisions already on this refugee journey. What we could do for Hanife was to listen, to care, and to bear witness to the God who sees and knows her situation, and who has himself entered our world, been a refugee, and been rejected. We bear witness to the One who knows Hanife, loves her, and wants to provide true refuge. We are only a small part in this big story. How will God use our kindness today in the long journey of Hanife's life? We may never know.

"Carol, you can't serve Jamila Noori with anything more than the medical care!" Joy was emphatic. She knew something of Jamila's story, and she knew of my soft heart toward Jamila.

Jamila had been coming to the program for over a decade now. Volunteers came and went; Jamila and I were fixtures. I knew her story. I had held her tears. Maybe it was her very small frame and her sad and aching widow's heart that moved me.

Jamila came to Turkey with her daughter and son-in-law. Her son-in-law wanted to escape the hardship and hopelessness of life in Afghanistan. He had been told that prospects were better in Turkey, that he would find work, healthcare, and education for his children. Friends had sent back glowing reports of the opportunities here and told him how glad they were to have migrated.

Jamila was widowed. Her husband had died in an accident, leaving her with two young children at home and three older children married with families of their own. Jamila went to live with her daughter's family along with her two youngest children, Sarah, age 10, and Musa, age 16. When her son-in-law decided to leave Afghanistan for Turkey, Jamila had little choice but to come along. She left behind her aging mother, also widowed, who lived with Jamila's sister. There was no other family that could take Jamila in, so she would have to go. It grieved her heart to leave. She left behind her older, married daughter, and four grandchildren. Her oldest son had not been heard from for some time, presumed dead in his own attempt to leave. The family of eight made the difficult journey from Afghanistan into Iran, across the mountains into eastern Turkey, and then across Turkey to Istanbul. We don't know exactly what they experienced, but we know from other accounts that the journey was difficult. Groups often reportedly travel by night to avoid being seen by any authorities. There were dangerous mountain passes to navigate. Some people had told us of family members who fell to their deaths on these treacherous journeys. Jamila was frail and vulnerable.

In Istanbul the family started by sharing an apartment with another family. They were crowded and the welcome soon wore off. Jamila's son-in-law found work, and they rented their own apartment near many other Afghan families. Jamila stayed home to cook, clean, and care for the children. Her daughter had given birth to her third child during the long journey to Turkey, and she was soon pregnant with a fourth.

Neighbors told Jamila and her daughter Bahara about an amazing place in central Istanbul where you could go. "You will receive help for things that you didn't even ask for!" they were told. One day Jamila and Bahara arrived together at our gate. On her first visit Jamila received a hot meal and vouchers to buy food at a neighborhood grocery store. Her children were seen by a nurse and given vitamins, and she was able to tell some of her story. She left thankful and returned the following week. We tried to explain to her that we had limits and could only see people at most once a month, but in the following years, Jamila became a frequent visitor to the program.

Jamila was not well. She complained of stomach problems, and her skin color was pale. We sent her to be evaluated at our partner hospital, Saint George. She was diagnosed with gastritis and returned to us with a long list of medications. Jamila is illiterate, so I coached her on when and how to take the medications by creating a color-coded chart. Over the many treatments in many years her symptoms would only disappear for a short period of time.

Jamila enjoyed coming to the center. She liked to eat a hot meal that someone else cooked. She liked to hear Bible stories. She took part in the creative arts projects, and, of course, she came inside to chat with the nurse. When her daughter Sarah finished school, Jamila no longer qualified for any of our financial aid programs, but her needs did not disappear. Instead, Jamila became the inspiration for our widow's assistance program.

The new program was a response to God's special concern for widows and orphans, and it allowed us to help widows with the cost of living once per year. This meant that my visits with Jamila were less frequent, but they would continue. On one visit I was surprised to learn that Jamila's mother had died, but that she had been unable to return for the funeral. She grieved deeply. We held each other and cried, our tears soaking into each other's shoulders. On another visit, I learned that one of her grandchildren in Afghanistan died in an accident. With loss upon loss, Jamila was navigating life with a broken heart.

Jamila represents for me what it means to show love and care for the vulnerable over the long haul. She showed such resilience, even though her face revealed the strains of life and loss. Will Jesus come to Jamila in a dream? If he does, she will already know his name, for she heard it often as we prayed with her in our small office. Will she respond to his call? That is my prayer.

Hope faced challenge after challenge in her decade-long stay as a Nigerian migrant in Turkey. Her husband, Robert, was in the import-export business but never gained legal status in Turkey. The couple worked hard in the face of deep prejudices.

Hope first came to us when she was pregnant. She was beaming with joy even as she grew uncomfortably large. She was carrying twins and would need to have a scheduled C-section at our partnering hospital. She gave birth to identical twin boys and returned to us bursting with pride. They grew and Hope handled all their energy with enthusiasm. She continued to be supported through our program for newborn care, having already received support for pregnancy and delivery.

We had not seen Hope for some months when we got a call from the hospital. She had appeared at the hospital late at night and told them to put her bill on our tab. Joshua, the older of her twins, had a high fever and suffered convulsions. Joshua was transferred to a pediatric ICU at another hospital. He was weeks, then months, in the hospital. His prolonged convulsions at the beginning of his illness had caused serious brain damage, and it was not clear what functions he would regain. He had multiple surgeries for complications with his airway and his stomach. Life was full of pressure, but Hope was a dedicated mother. She sought to do all she could for both Joshua and Jacob. When you are already living on the edge and catastrophic events occur, you have no buffer to soften the trauma. Hope's commitment to her family and her persevering hope in the face of these circumstances was admirable and humbling.

Hope cared for Joshua at great personal sacrifice. She sought out resources to make the care easier and spoke with numerous agencies to leverage all the support that she could. It was not clear to any of us how much function Joshua would regain, but Hope was going to give him every chance. Jacob grew and his energy was boundless. He was a constant visual stimulus for Joshua. Hope managed both boys remarkably well and seemingly tirelessly. Hope was designated by our board to receive extra support from our program due to the severity of their circumstances. She came often, and we stayed updated on the progress, no matter how small.

One day Hope appeared at our gate with Joshua. She was wearing dark glasses. Robert had snapped. He couldn't take any more - so many months with higher costs, never alone with Hope, always trying to provide but never being able to do enough. Hope's work was at home, and that was a drain on their income, not a help. Robert hit her in an outburst of rage. He had not hit Joshua, and he had never done this before. "What can I do?" was Hope's cry for help. She was a fighter, but this was too much. "I can't stay with him, but I can't leave him. What do I do?"

We counseled her that he needed help, and together they should seek counseling, but Robert was unwilling. He could not take the stress. When he tried to hit Hope a second time, she told him to leave; he was not welcome.

Not long after, he returned. He was sorry, he said. It would not happen again. Hope let him come home. But the cycle recurred, until a final episode became too much. Hope had other single women live with her to help with the rent. She shared a room with the boys. On one visit to the center, I gently asked about the sustainability of her situation and initiated a conversation about repatriation. Would she consider taking the boys home to Nigeria? We would help to obtain passports for all of them, since Hope's was long expired. Along with the International Organization for Migration (IOM), we could help her to leave and have a fresh start. "No" was always her answer. Turkey was hard, but Nigeria would be harder. The choice was hers to make. We were called to respect and support her, but we also could not sustain her here.

Hanife, Jamila, and Hope carry different burdens, yet each was seen, heard, and accompanied. Our resources were limited; God's were not. Where our help ended, his faithful care continued with the assurance that though alone, they were not unseen.

Soraya, a 35-year-old Afghan woman, sat in front of me asking for help. She had come to Turkey a year earlier, with her four-year-old son and four-month-old daughter. Her husband had come ahead. When she arrived, she found that he had taken another wife and wanted nothing to do with her or her children. He had supported her journey out of Afghanistan, knowing that it was a mercy for her to leave, but he had revealed nothing of his new marriage. Devastated, she was left on her own, struggling to survive. Eight months later her one-year-old daughter was injured in her home and died in the hospital. When she learned that her daughter had died, Soraya fell to the ground in shock and lost four front teeth. We first met her following 40 days of mourning, when a neighbor brought her to us for help.

What could I say? What could I do to come alongside Soraya in her pain? Her suffering seemed unbearable. How do we enter into such suffering? Grief and loss followed by more grief and more loss. Soraya could barely function; she hardly felt alive anymore. Grief and abandonment are like living in a dark room with the lights turned out. Sometimes such feelings can be so deeply felt in the body that one feels it all the time or does not feel it at all. Is it possible to "adapt"?

So much of what we try to do with refugees involves coming alongside them in impossible situations like Soraya's – slowly, gently, prayerfully, and humbly. We cannot erase the past or restore what has been lost, but we can bear witness to suffering and refuse to let it be borne alone. Like Jesus, we can be present to listen and to weep, and we can refuse to turn away. Ultimately, we long for those like Soraya to find refuge in the one unshakeable hope.

Hanife, Jamila, Hope, and Soraya are all vulnerable, unprotected women, alone and abandoned in their journey, reflecting our focus on vulnerable women in recent years. But in the program's early years, it was African men who needed help.

Africans have migrated to Turkey for decades, often hoping it will be a bridge to Europe. After reaching Turkey, often after a grueling journey through North Africa and the Middle East, many face shock and disillusionment as they struggle just to survive and to evade detention or deportation. In the first two years of the program, coordinators spent long hours visiting African migrants in prison and seeking legal help to have them released. In the early 1990s, undocumented African migrants were often rounded up and sent to detention camps far from Istanbul, near the border with Iraq. An early coordinator described the dire situation of more than 160 men detained in Silopi. Board members arranged for clothes, blankets, food, and medicine to be delivered to them and visited them in the detention camp.

Other migrants were transported to Turkey's western border, released, and told to walk across into Greece. In 1995, six Tanzanian men were detained in Istanbul. Two had passports, but the police rejected them as falsified. They were handcuffed, blindfolded, put on a minibus, and driven to the Greek border. On arrival, late at night, they were released, their blindfolds were removed, and they were forced at gunpoint to walk across empty fields towards the Greek border. The fields were dense with landmines. We can easily imagine that these six were the fortunate ones. After entering Greece they were detained, strip searched, rough-handled, and sent back to Turkey across the same border. The coordinator reported that “they were forced to cross to and fro eight times during a period of a month, each time at night, each time in cold and dangerous conditions.”

Finally a Turkish villager found them lying in a ditch. He called a taxi to take them to Edirne, the closest city, and from there they were returned to an Istanbul prison by police transport.

Our program coordinator was contacted and asked to visit these men. It was not his first time to make such a visit. He took clothes and toiletries to the prisoners, and they were given time to talk. They received compassionate care and the promise of advocacy. A few of them needed medical assistance which was arranged and paid for by the program. Others perished in the border minefields. The coordinator wrote, “During this period, I know of two Africans who have died in no man's land, and two who have been injured. Two were buried in Orestiada (Greece) on 31 January 1995 – one unknown, the other Machubu Victor from Rwanda (b. 1970). Two others are in Greek hospitals with severe injuries.”

Circumstances like these motivated the program's board to form a separate NGO focused entirely on providing legal assistance. Legal advocacy required time and specialized resources, and was better separated from the physical, social and psychological care for the sick, the hungry, and the poor. Coordinators could not focus well on both. Staff from the center contributed to the establishment of a dedicated legal-aid initiative in Turkey. This evolved over the 2000s into RLAP and then into HCA-RASP under the Helsinki Citizens' Assembly, eventually becoming today's Refugee Rights Turkey, which remains Turkey's leading legal NGO serving refugees. Refugee Rights Turkey continues to be an essential partner to our church-based refugee program, offering a valuable option for referral of those whose rights have been ignored or violated.

While faces and stories have changed over time, the heart of the work remains the same. From the early days of prison visits to African men, to the present focus on vulnerable women like Hanife, Jamila, Hope, and Soraya, our small one-room office has been a sanctuary for the vulnerable, unprotected, and abandoned to share stories like these. For a brief time, they are offered love, care, respect, and protection, and they can let down their guard. At the same time, it is a place where we, as volunteers, willingly allow pain to enter our own hearts and minds; we take on the weight of these stories often without knowing how they end. The stories intrude on our sleep, imprint images of pain on our memories. Later we will return to the challenges of unfinished stories and strategies for caring over time.

As the work has changed in scope and focus, with new programs, new partnerships, and new forms of advocacy, changes have required flexibility, creativity, and faith. Every situation is different; every encounter brings its own unanticipated challenges and difficult choices. There are no manuals for compassion. The next chapter turns to stories that illustrate how volunteers and coordinators have needed imagination, flexibility, and endurance to deal with unexpected challenges.

Adaptability

Let the favor of the Lord our God be upon us,

and establish the work of our hands upon us;

yes, establish the work of our hands!

Psalm 90:17

"How do we dispose of this Tramadol?" Sue asked me. She knew that I had worked in community hospice care. My training had given me experience disposing of narcotics; I knew how to make drugs unusable and undesirable for humans or animals before they are thrown in the trash.

Naïve but well-intentioned volunteers and friends of the program donated all manner of things. The office heaved at times under the weight of bags and boxes of donated belongings. This may have been one of the motives for the creation of a clothing cupboard for refugees and migrants. It took another army of volunteers to oversee the organization and distribution of donated clothing.

But disposing of donated narcotics was a special problem. I offered to meet Sue at the office on a day when the center was closed.

The day Sue and I met, rain was pouring down, puddles were growing, and the drains in the garden could not keep up with the heavy downpour. Sue and I, inside the office, were on our knees with a hammer and pills between us. Beside us were two large zip-lock bags with a mixture of cat litter, coffee grounds, and wet oatmeal. As we leaned over, crushing pills and putting the powder in the bags, Sue surprised me with an unexpected question. Would I consider taking on the role of coordinator? She was resigning in the coming months. I was shocked and humbled, and I could immediately see the magnitude of the challenge. I had often said, as I sat at the desk next to Sue, "I have no idea how you do what you do. I could never do your job!"

Sue sensed my surprise. "Take your time thinking this over," she said. "I know that when I started, I felt very overwhelmed. That is normal. But I am confident that you can do this. And you need to know, it is the best work I have done in my career."

When we left the office, with the garbage bags in our hands, it was still raining. Now we had the challenge of disposing of them. I was lost in thought as we moved together up the narrow passageway leading to the street. We had shared a secret, bonding adventure, and now we had a plan, but I faced an unexpected decision. We moved nonchalantly, past multiple security cameras, in the direction of the dumpsters. Each of us took turns flinging our garbage bag high over the side, then we walked confidently toward the tramway, mission accomplished. The drugs had been rendered unusable. And a new chapter would begin for me.

From the program's beginnings in the 1990s, participating churches have often sponsored their own specialized programs for refugees and migrants. These have included language classes, soup kitchens, programs for social needs, and job training. Turkish language programs have served refugees staying in Turkey. Those designated for resettlement have sometimes been offered French, English or German instruction. Soup kitchens on different days organized by different parishes provide both food and community. Clothing cupboards in varied locations on different days serve practical needs. Some parishes sponsored computer literacy classes to assist in employment. Game nights were hosted to combat isolation and loneliness. The range of services offered over the years has far exceeded the capacity of any one parish. Nor could our center have organized it all. What no single church could accomplish alone became possible through the shared vision, cooperation, and full commitment of all our partner churches.

The Moms and Tots program at the Union Church was one such initiative that continues. The program was launched as a meeting place for young mothers, providing a warm meal and a place where relationships could be nurtured. Union Church began to host Moms and Tots in 2004. Over time, the program grew to serve multiple nationalities and languages, including English, French, Arabic, and Dari. Its volunteers also focus on home visits to establish relationships and engage more holistically in the participating women's lives. Moms and Tots has coordinated closely with the center, preventing duplication of services and allowing referrals back and forth.

For many years the Ecumenical Patriarchate of the Greek Orthodox Church offered a soup kitchen near Taksim Square in the heart of the city. "Whatever you do," Sue had warned me, "don't let the Greek Orthodox soup kitchen close!" Her words instilled fear in me as she passed responsibility to me. The Taksim soup kitchen was the Ecumenical Patriarchate's primary contribution; we did not want to lose their involvement. But the program was at risk. The assistant to the coordinator who had overseen the program had left Istanbul. The program was hosted in the lovely garden of the Aya Triada Church. The garden was a peaceful haven for families, but its location in the heart of the city meant increased surveillance and intense police presence. The year I took over as coordinator, Istanbul endured multiple bombings and an attempted coup.

"How can I prevent this part of the program from closing?" I had been wondering, anxiously. Then the fateful call came. "We are no longer going to prepare food for the soup kitchen. Refugees are not attending." Despite my efforts, the gates were closing. Risks beyond my control had driven refugees away, and volunteers were weary of preparing food for no one to claim. We needed a creative solution.

When our programs started up again the next fall, I had a brainstorm. Would the Ecumenical Patriarchate be willing to bring food to our office garden on a day when refugees are already present? They would not be hosting at their facility, but they could contribute the cooking, and our volunteers would serve it. "Yes, good plan!" came the response. The partnership with the Patriarchate continues, and a representative of the Patriarchate recently served as chair of the board.

Crises and challenges, large and small, required the same flexibility and resilience that we so often saw in those for whom we served. Over time I came to think of the program as a three-legged stool, supported by those we served, those who volunteered, and donors who made it possible to fund our services. When any of those three was off-kilter, we needed to adapt to restore balance.

Some seasons brought silence; others, chaos. The summer of 2015 taught us how to wait when families had moved on toward Europe leaving our garden empty. Five years later, the pandemic taught us how to cope when crowds arrived at our gate and social-distancing rules made gathering impossible. In both extremes we had to listen, pray, and redesign.

We thought there would never be a shortage of people to serve. The numbers and needs of those who came to Istanbul from all over the world – the poor, the needy, the refugees, widows, orphans – would always exceed our capacity. We learned differently during the mass migration of 2015. The line of women waiting outside our gate evaporated. We had volunteers, we had funds, and we had food, but we had no one to receive them.

For weeks our volunteers sat in the garden with hardly anyone to serve. Many of those who came to us had seized the opportunity to leave Turkey, seeking a better future further along the refugee highway, even if that meant risking their lives at sea or spending months in a camp. We read headlines about tragedies at sea as overloaded, unseaworthy boats went down. But we could only wait, pray, and feel the eerie sense of loss as days turned into weeks and still no one came.

As Istanbul emptied, Europe flooded. Hundreds of thousands joined a huge wave of migrants on land and sea. A miles-long migrant caravan traveled on foot through Greece and Bulgaria, Hungary and Austria. By sea, a steady stream of life rafts arrived on Greek islands and Italian beaches. One of our partner churches that year set up an Advent crèche calculated to shock: The Holy Family wore life jackets. The crèche was a powerful image of lives at risk, of the displacement and arduous journey of Mary and Joseph, and of the meaning of the Incarnation.

The 2015 mass migration was short-lived. Borders closed. Nations collaborated to keep refugees where they were. Turkey and Lebanon would continue to bear the brunt of the burden.

A few years later, Covid-19 brought the opposite challenge. When we opened for our second day after a four-month closure in 2020, we were met with an overwhelming crush of need. The first day had gone smoothly. On this second day, we expected a larger crowd, but we felt ready. We would distribute cards of different colors to each group of 12 women; the color would indicate the time that each should return to the gate to be admitted. We could not allow crowding at the gate, or waiting on the street. Both the Turkish government and our host church had introduced strict social-distancing protocols.

We knew we had entered crisis mode when an urgent message came from the gate. "There are too many women!" More than 90 were crowding the gate, pushing each other, ignoring instructions. Desperation and fear of missing out on help seemed to be causing a riot. Then police arrived and began videoing. They demanded to know who was instigating the chaos. In the face of a growing emergency, our astute Turkish gatekeeper took charge. He raised his cane in the air and yelled out, "What are you doing? You should be ashamed! This is Turkey. This is a land of law and order!" His quick intervention bought us time to close the gate, and satisfied the police that the situation was under control. The crowd dispersed, but it was clear that our systems could not cope with the new reality. We were forced to shut down after serving only 19 women.

I was sad and confused. The refugees we wanted to serve were desperate; we had resources to share; but the desperation made distribution impossible. The experience was all too similar to what aid workers frequently experience in crisis environments; it was like driving a truck full of food into a village filled with starving people. We had to regroup, plan, and adapt. We prayed, and we met to troubleshoot. Should we move our location? Should we change the day we are open? Refugees would learn about any change with lightning speed, and crowds would quickly gather again.

Necessity and smartphones inspired invention. Almost every refugee family has access to a smartphone; they are essential to survival on the arduous migrant journey. That evening we bought an available website address and quickly set up a rudimentary website linked to our database. A simple form in Turkish, Persian, and English would allow refugees to register, and would allow us to call them in for appointments. Miraculously, the plan worked and we reopened. By God's grace and thanks to generous donations from around the world, two days a week for the next six weeks, we served 500 families with basic emergency cash and food coupons.

The system worked smoothly. Translators shifted from in-person interviews at the center to making phone calls to tell people to come in on a specific date at a particular time. They sometimes reached a phone number shared by multiple people. When our Persian translator called one client, she reached the woman's husband. "Wait one minute! Stay on the line!" he told her. "I am at work, but I'll run home and get my wife!" Those we served quickly adapted to the protocol; we were able to serve a limited number each day and never again faced overwhelming crowds. The appointment system is still in use.

The pandemic brought other challenges. Treating those who came to us with compassion required that we avoid exposing them or our volunteers to risk of exposure through long interviews or close contact. No matter how desperate the circumstances, we limited our care to a standard emergency aid package. There were no hugs. Women were appreciative of the help, but they clearly had losses they wanted to process. It was a sterile season, but we were open and meeting in person.

Adaptability begins with those we serve, but it also depends on those willing to serve. A volunteer-based program changes daily. Text messages – "I'm sick," "I'm traveling," "A team is visiting" – reshaped each morning. At any point a volunteer may have something else to do or somewhere else to be. "I am sorry, I am not feeling well. I will not be at the program today." "I am going on a trip for a month and won't be back until sometime after my return. I will let you know when." Or, "My church has a team of six that are coming to see what we do. Can they come with me to the center this morning?" Our schedule had to flex, priorities to adjust. Coordinating required flexibility and humor. But it has also been an amazing privilege to witness the commitment and care of an ever-widening global family of highly skilled and deeply compassionate volunteers over the years. My colleagues frequently offered great grace to me as I led, and they have served with love, skill, and deep humility.

Some moments stand out. The humble service of our volunteers was especially moving. One of our highly skilled nurses saw another volunteer sweeping the garden one morning. She shared her concern with me. "Don't you think it is a waste of his skills?" she objected. "With his years of study, how can he be sweeping the garden?" She knew Albert's professional skills. He was a Brazilian lawyer who wanted to serve refugees. We had connected him with our legal aid partners at Refugee Rights Turkey, but he wanted to do more. He wanted to learn, observe, hear stories, and serve. Albert was willing to do anything that needed to be done. At the start of the day, he swept the garden. At lunch he served hot food. He helped at the gate with security. During interviews he sat listening to refugee stories. All the while he was doing research in his spare time to understand what it looks like to sponsor refugees, and he was becoming familiar with refugee service organizations like the IOM. The experience bore fruit. Albert returned to Brazil after six weeks at our program, six weeks at another church-based program in another city, and six weeks on a Greek island at a refugee camp. After he returned home to Brazil, he formed an NGO to advocate for refugee resettlement. For more than seven years, he has been using his legal skills to equip Brazilians to better welcome refugees.

Our nurse was not so different. She saw Albert through maternal eyes: what would his mother think to see what he was doing in Istanbul? But she herself was also willing to do any job that needed doing, including cleaning bathrooms. I often saw in our volunteers the servanthood that we see in Christ. Our shared goal was to imitate him, the creator and sustainer of the universe, who knelt down and washed the feet of his friends, who touched the unclean and took on their uncleanness.

I think of our volunteers as weaving together a rich tapestry of skill, compassion, and commitment. Were we to assign a monetary value to the countless hours of service donated by skilled lawyers, nurses, midwives, doctors, engineers, teachers, social workers, physical therapists, occupational therapists, counselors, artists, graduate students, linguists, administrators, retirees, pastors, retired military officers, and computer technicians, the sum would be beyond calculation. God has brought all walks of life to serve together. Some came only for a day, but that day has lingered with them for decades. Others served for years.

One of our critical needs was for good gatekeepers. Many mornings when I arrived at the office, I found women and children sitting on the outer steps of the church building waiting for the outside gate to be opened.

This often meant that the long passageway to our inner gate was already full. I sometimes had to press through the crowd to unlock the garden gate at the end of the long passage. Because I was alone, I could not let any of them enter; it was too early to decide how many we would serve or who from the crowd qualified. I had to wait for a translator to make those decisions. Yet it was painful to shut the gate behind me and to work alone in my office with a crowd of more than 30 women waiting with their children.

After volunteers arrived and we could assess our capacity for the day, I returned to the gate with a translator to give out numbers. "Lord, help!" I often prayed, as I walked the 30 meters from my desk to the gate, "Give me your wisdom and compassion." The decisions were difficult, but they had to be made quickly. For those new to the program there would be a different set of questions. Newcomers often came with high expectations. Sometimes they learned of our program in a park from a fellow refugee. "Go there, they will help you." Some women arrived thinking that we were UNICEF or the United Nations. We asked questions of each newcomer: Are you pregnant? Do you have small children? The questions would communicate our priorities and limitations to newcomers. But they could sometimes cause people to misrepresent their situation to gain entry.

Each one who came had need; that much was clear. But we could not help them all. We needed to be faithful to the purpose of the program, to be wise and to be generous.

For many years Klaus was one of our most faithful volunteers. He was a retired German military officer; his wife taught at the German school in Istanbul. Klaus learned of our program at the German Lutheran Church in Istanbul, and he volunteered to serve as our gatekeeper. It was often a cold, wet, and thankless job, yet the task was critical to keep the program running smoothly and to maintain the safety of our volunteers and those for whom they cared. For 28 years, we had an open gate. Sometimes we were the only program in Istanbul where a refugee could show up and hope to receive help without an appointment. But this required careful management. Klaus understood our limitations. When a refugee came to the gate with a request, he immediately knew if it was beyond our capacity. Klaus served refugees by not wasting their time with false expectations; he served other volunteers by enabling us to use resources more effectively; he served God by doing his work graciously.

Managing crowds of people with compassion and wisdom was one part of the gatekeeping. Gatekeepers also needed to understand our priorities and limitations. A woman who was registered with us arrived one morning with a young man who was a stranger to her. She knew that we serve undocumented migrants. I was called to the gate to make a judgment about whether to allow him to come in and be seen. We had already distributed all of our numbers for the day. But I immediately saw that the young man was very sick. He needed more care than we could provide. My task was to urge him to go immediately to a hospital. He was reluctant out of fear that he would be refused care. We gave taxi money and directed him to the nearest emergency room.

The third leg of the three-legged stool, funding, also required careful stewardship. Too little was a problem; so was too much. "You should be asking for more money this year on this grant," the chair of our board once told me. "We qualify for it, and the foundation is very pleased with our programs." But it wasn't so simple. What would happen when the grant ended? Would we be able to sustain the programs that expanded because of it? Partly for this reason, the board has been committed to funding the ongoing, core budget of the program from the donations of our partner churches in Istanbul.

At times, however, grants have funded especially valuable programs. After 2011, when a wave of Syrian refugees came to Istanbul, wise volunteers recognized a special need. Syrian children were allowed to enroll in Turkish schools, but how could parents be encouraged to keep them out of the workforce and off the streets and to invest in their education? The creative response was to expand our Children's Education program, which provided financial incentives to families who could show that their children remained enrolled in school. A few years later, when a program for Syrians similar to ours was funded by the EU, we quickly adapted our program. We gave the Syrians a full year's notice that our support of their schooling was ending and instructed them on how to register for this much larger program. We then switched the focus of our program to Afghans. But even multi-year grant programs come to an end. When the third year of the grant is completed, we are left on the edge of a precipice. Programs reduce in size and require new criteria.

Sometimes small crises arose by surprise. One day an official from the electric company arrived outside our building. He was preparing to cut a cable, when our gatekeeper asked him what he was doing. "We are here to cut the electricity to the garden building," he replied. I was called to the scene. Our bill was in arrears, the official told me. I also learned that the bill was still in the name of the second coordinator of the program who had been gone from Istanbul 23 years! "What can I do to keep the electricity on?" I asked the man with wire cutters in his hand. I promised him that the bill would be paid by the end of the day. We learned our lesson and put the bill on an automatic payment plan.

An Australian visitor to the program who had worked in many different church settings, marveled at the ways that our program brought diverse churches together. There are few places in the world where such a wide range of churches have worked together so closely for so many years. The challenges are huge. Cultures differ, resources differ, priorities differ, but all agree that the call to follow Christ in the care of "the least of these" is the shared call of the whole church, and of every church. This clarity has helped us through the moments of strain.

At one of my first board meetings, after two board members broke into a sharp disagreement in a language that I did not understand and one member stormed out in anger, I truly wondered what I had gotten myself into by leading the program. When doors were locked without warning, denying access to bathrooms for any of the volunteers or visitors to the garden, we had to approach the challenge with the same adaptability with which we faced other crises. When the rent was raised beyond our ability to pay, it took long hours of agonizing meetings and communication. It was an opportunity to remind our church partners of the common calling to serve the poor.

The need to adapt to circumstances and challenges did not change our calling; it was a requirement of it. On some days the garden was silent; on others it roared. Volunteers came and went; grants started and ended; gates opened and closed; and appointment lists replaced lines. Yet through each change, the work continued because the God who sees kept watch over us.

God is our refuge and strength, a very present help in trouble … "Be still, and know that I am God."

Psalm 46:1, 10

Binta was ill with a fever and needed help. A thirty-five-year-old Gambian migrant, she was recovering from a radical mastectomy and would soon start chemotherapy for breast cancer. Binta was married and had a one-year-old son, Mohammed. I was reluctant to make the long journey across the city to her apartment in Kumkapı, but I knew she needed a visit.

We had cared for Binta for several months. She had first come to us pregnant, then postpartum, then with the complaint of a painful breast lump. We paid for a biopsy followed by a full mastectomy. Now she would need chemotherapy followed by radiation. A cancer diagnosis is a crisis for any of us; it was an especially intense crisis for Binta. By faith, we had committed to carry the costs of her treatment as long as we could. We made it clear that this was too big for us, but not too big for God. We would help Binta as God provided the resources, one step at a time.

Neither Binta nor her husband was documented. Their passports were expired and they had no residence permit to be in the country. Employment for each of them had been unstable. They had a nine-year-old daughter back in Gambia who was living with Binta's mother. Return to Gambia was not an option; adequate treatment would be unavailable to Binta there.

Kumkapı is a rough neighborhood, even during the daytime. Binta and her husband offset their rent by sharing their apartment with migrant workers. She provided me with the address, and Dan and I climbed three flights of dark, narrow stairs. He was coming with me both for safety in the neighborhood and to help if something needed to be purchased from a local shop. A Senegalese man who spoke only French answered the door and guided us to Binta's room. Binta, her husband, and their son lived in a small south-facing room that overlooked other rooftops in the densely crowded neighborhood. Eight single men shared two other bedrooms, four in each room. The men would come and go to work, both day and night. Moussa, Binta's husband, also had an unpredictable schedule. He was not home when we visited. Binta did most of the cooking for everyone in the apartment, and she shared one small bathroom with her husband and eight other men. We brought Binta groceries, made her tea, and talked about the need for rest, fluids, and attention to nutrition. We sat on the bed and played with Mohammed so that Binta could have some time to wash herself. Her fever had broken, and she wanted to feel refreshed. We read the stories of Jairus' sick daughter and the woman with bleeding from chapter five of Mark's Gospel. Binta needed God's healing touch. Binta also needed her mother to come and care for her and for all the other men to leave. But that would not be happening. The visit gave me a vivid sense of her everyday world, and I came away prayerful and humbled.

Three weeks later Binta and I spent days at the hospital for screening tests in preparation for her chemotherapy. I was her medical advocate and Turkish interpreter. Though my Turkish was not nearly fluent, it was better than no Turkish at all. Binta spoke only English and Wolof.

Together we began to see God open doors and show his care for her through the generosity of caregivers. The oncologist cared for Binta with uncommon kindness, giving more of himself than his role required. The receptionist came to know us and was eager to troubleshoot challenges for us. A Turkish patient, who had recently completed her cancer journey, showed deep sympathy to Binta. When their paths would cross, she would help Binta to navigate layers of testing in areas of the hospital where I was not allowed to enter.

It was the middle of summer when I boarded the metrobus to meet Binta for her fourth chemotherapy session at the government hospital. The day was hot, and the metrobus is my least favorite form of transportation in Istanbul. It is an amazing and efficient way of moving large numbers of people long distances through the city at low cost. But it is crowded! Those who board at the beginning of the route might have a seat, but I usually boarded at a later station where the buses arrived already crowded. The walk up stairs and across bridges to the platforms, which are usually in the median of the highway, are long, hot, and tiring. I remember working to convince myself to keep going on this miserable journey, packed in a bus, by remembering how Jesus, God incarnate, lowered himself to human form and suffered the pains of our world to save us. Surely I could make this small journey to show up for Binta and to care for her in her pain.

Binta was waiting for me when I arrived. I was surprised to also see Mohammed. She had not succeeded in finding childcare. That meant that I needed to stay all day, caring for Mohammed without any easy place to take him.

We began the long, complex process of registering Binta to see the doctor. When we reached the doctor's office, I left for the cashier to pay any remaining balance. I had come prepared. When I reached the cashier, I was surprised to learn that Binta's balance was much higher than I had experienced before or anticipated this time. Her previous treatment had included extra costs for testing. I didn't have enough money with me, and her treatment could not continue until her bill was paid. I had no other way to pay her debt. I made my way back to the doctor's office, defeated. I entered the office to report that we would have to delay the treatment because I didn't have the resources to pay the debt on Binta's account. An oncology intern who was working with the doctor and who knew us from previous appointments asked to speak to Binta and me outside the office. We stepped into an adjoining room. He reached into his wallet and passed me ten one-hundred-dollar bills. I was stunned! "I want to help," he said in broken English. "Please go and pay the bill."

Quickly and excitedly, I left the office to go and exchange the money while Binta waited with Mohammad. I walked into the neighborhood of the hospital with urgency, searching for a currency exchange. There were none. I found a goldsmith shop. I had heard that goldsmiths sometimes changed money. The goldsmith exchanged eight bills for me; two were too old to be accepted. I settled Binta's account and returned to find her in the waiting room. Binta's chemo treatment proceeded that day, and I had a fresh sense of God's hand at work and renewed energy to care for Mohammed during her treatment.

When Binta finally emerged from treatment, I asked her, "So how do you feel?"

"I'm fine," she said, without emotion. I was surprised. Of course, she had just come out of a chemo treatment and was facing a long journey back to her apartment on public transport with Mohammed. But she had just received an unexpected gift from a stranger! "Just fine?" I probed. Tears came to Binta's eyes, and the painful backstory spilled out. "Moussa tells me that this is all because of my sin. It is my fault that I am sick."

"No, Binta!" I exclaimed. "Illness and death happen to all of us! Sin has broken creation, but we have a savior, a rescuer. The rescuer showed up today in your story, Binta! Today is not about your cancer or your sin! Today God showed you his amazing love for you. He arranged to pay your bill today the same way that he has paid the debt for your sin through the life, death, and resurrection of his Son, Jesus. Our powerful, loving God who is here, who knows you, who cares for you, and who wants you to know him is your rescuer." My words were filled with passion, maybe too much passion. Truth tumbled out, and I was in awe of what God had done, and I wanted Binta to be in awe. I wanted her to see the love of God.

Binta went on to have four more chemo treatments and then began targeted radiation. The treatment plan called for 26 radiation treatments; after 24 treatments, Binta went silent. We had no idea where she had gone. A few weeks later Binta sent me a WhatsApp message. She had arrived in Germany. We were stunned. Sometimes migrants talk to us about hiring smugglers to reach Europe. But Binta had never mentioned leaving. And when she left, she took Mohammed with her but left without Moussa. She had not felt loved through her long journey with cancer, and she chose to leave Turkey without him.

Over time I lost track of Binta. Is she back in the Gambia? Still in Germany? I don't know. But God does – and I continue to pray that she knows and responds to his overwhelming love. Her crisis was one that God had clearly provided for, and we witnessed his kindness to her again and again through every stage of her journey.

Behind every migration statistic are faces, names, and stories. The reasons people flee are many – danger, violence, war, famine, floods, persecution – but each journey begins in crisis, and many, like Binta, face new crises in the very places where they seek refuge. According to the United Nations High Commissioner for Refugees (UNHCR), "A refugee is someone who has been forced to flee his or her country because of persecution, war or violence. A refugee has a well-founded fear of persecution for reasons of race, religion, nationality, political opinion or membership in a particular social group. Most likely, they cannot return home or are afraid to do so. War and violence – ethnic, tribal, religious – are leading causes of refugees fleeing their countries" (unrefugees.org/refugee-facts/what-is-a-refugee).

This story is not new. Humans have fled crisis since the beginning; migration runs through the whole biblical story. From the moment Adam and Eve were driven from Eden, humanity has been on the move, seeking refuge and rest. Cain, the first murderer, became a restless wanderer. Abraham left home and kin to live as a foreigner in a strange land. Hagar twice fled Sarah's cruelty; each time God met her in the wilderness, first to send her back, later to save her and her son. Rebekah left her homeland to marry Isaac. Jacob fled his brother's rage to find safety with family abroad. Joseph was sold into slavery by jealous brothers, yet God turned his captivity to provide refuge for his family. Generations later they became slaves until God again delivered them from bondage into freedom. Naomi fled famine in Israel for Moab; David hid in caves from Saul's spear; centuries later, Israel's rebellion led to exile in Babylon. Mary and Joseph fled to Egypt with the infant Jesus, seeking refuge from Herod's violence.

Following Jesus' death, resurrection and ascension, his followers were scattered and dispersed, aliens and strangers on earth. The biblical narrative is a story of people on the move – refugees, migrants, foreigners, strangers.

God's mandate to his people to care for the refugees and foreigners in our midst makes much better sense when we see it as a part of this story to which all of us belong. From the beginning, God instructed Israel, "You shall love the stranger, for you were strangers in the land of Egypt" (Deut 10:19; cf. Ex 22:21; Lev 19:33–34). Compassion was to flow from the realization that they had been aliens themselves. None of us belong; we are aliens and strangers on the earth (1 Peter 2:11; Hebrews 11:13). We are strangers called to care for strangers, aliens called to care for aliens. Ignoring refugees is not an option for the people of God.

The challenge must be faced anew in each generation. In a single decade the number of displaced persons has more than doubled, increasing from 60 million to 120 million. Nations may build walls to keep out the refugees and migrants; governments and political parties may retreat to nationalism and nativism. The Church has a different mandate.

"A woman in the park told me to come here for help," Miriam told me. She had arrived in Istanbul just three days before. "My husband is looking for work. I'm expecting a baby, and I need to see a doctor." Young and a foreigner in an unfamiliar world, Miriam was grateful for any help we could give her. She had little education and understood little about what to expect of pregnancy and birth.

We set up an appointment for Miriam to return the following week and to go with one of our translators for a prenatal appointment. Miriam arrived at the gate in visible discomfort on the day of her appointment. Her husband was with her. What was wrong? Miriam told us that she had been to an emergency room early that morning. Both she and her husband had woken before dawn. He was attentive and boiled water for her to use in the shower so that she would be clean when she was seen by the doctor. Some of the very hot water tipped onto her in the shower, and she suffered second- and third-degree burns. Miriam's husband took her to the ER, where she was cared for and bandaged. Despite her injury and pain, she wanted to have her prenatal appointment, so she traveled a full hour to our center. Her resolve was both moving and sad.

Miriam's husband showed great care for her through the remaining months of her pregnancy. He always accompanied her to her appointments. She delivered a beautiful baby girl. After the delivery they came together to our office, beaming with joy. This fragile family was wrapped in love. We reimbursed a portion of their birth costs and coached Miriam on breastfeeding.

A year later, Miriam returned, pregnant again. Both she and her husband were excited. Life is not easy, but children are a blessing. The pregnancy progressed well. But on a November morning Miriam entered our office carrying a full bundle. Her face was no longer radiant. "Something is not right," she told me. I unwrapped the bundle; her beautifully formed son was alert and responsive. "What is wrong?" I asked.

Miriam took off the baby's outer layer and showed me his right arm. It hung limp at his side, unresponsive. My heart sank. To be born into a refugee family often begins a lifelong struggle; add to that a severe disability, and it seemed more than any young family could bear.

As Miriam described her difficult birth experience, my sadness turned to anger. Her labor had been difficult, and when the baby's shoulders were stuck in the birth canal the doctors had rushed the delivery causing severe nerve damage to the baby's arm. The doctors had ordered x-rays and had then told Miriam that, "Everything is okay. The bones are not broken." They refused to take any responsibility, or to follow up. But everything was not OK. Because they were undocumented, the couple was charged a higher rate for the difficult delivery, and now they were not welcome back to the private hospital. Vulnerable and undocumented, Miriam and her husband had little recourse.

A birth injury is a crisis for any child and family, but for a refugee it becomes a burden far beyond their capacity to bear. A volunteer from a partner program took this young family under his care. He established a good long-term relationship with Miriam's husband. He invested in the child's care. He raised money to cover the cost of physical therapy every month for many months. We saw little improvement but continued to hope.

Miriam and her husband care well for each other and for their children. They have worked hard to obtain residence documentation. Miriam's husband works hard to provide. They have been tempted to make the risky entry into Europe, hoping that surgery might be available there. But they are still in Istanbul at the time of writing.

Miriam's husband willingly takes time away from work to go to specialist appointments with his son, hoping that something can be done. Surgery is possible but offers no guarantees. At best, limb function might improve by 30 percent. The expense is overwhelming, well beyond the reach of a refugee family, or the resources of our center. Miriam and her husband have accepted these circumstances. We came alongside them in many ways at the center. We communicate our care each time that we see Miriam. Young Yusuf has the tremendous blessing of a loving family. Miriam's story reminds me that crisis reveals not only need but courage.

Refugee families like hers show us what it means to live with dignity when almost everything else is uncertain. This is a gift that will follow Yusuf as he grows, despite his disability.

Arzu had been in Istanbul for three months and was very early in her second pregnancy. Her 13-month-old son played near the table as she told us about her harrowing journey to Istanbul. It was early winter, and Arzu had only a thin sweater to cover her underweight frame. One of our volunteers lived nearby. She had a knee-length coat that she had just replaced with a newer version of the same. She ran home to get it and returned to give it to Arzu. Sometimes acts of spontaneous generosity like this are unwise because they set up unreasonable expectations for others. But on this day, Arzu was the last client present in the garden.

We cared for Arzu during her pregnancy. She visited the hospital for two prenatal visits. During that time her husband was hired to work in a textile factory. They were able to move out of the apartment they had shared with another small Afghan family. Arzu's growing pregnant body made her walk more slowly than her energetic, growing toddler. "Do you know where you will deliver?" I asked her. This was a routine question when we counseled pregnant women. The women who come to us need to make their own plans and find a place close to where they live to go when they are in labor. Her first labor, in Afghanistan, had been relatively easy. Her son had been delivered by a midwife. We coached her to not go to the private hospital because the fees would be high. But it would be her decision.

Three weeks later, Arzu returned. Her face betrayed her distress. She unwrapped the blankets around her newborn son, revealing a cleft lip. She was fearful and overwhelmed. Her infant son was able to nurse, but it was difficult. I tried to reassure Arzu. A cleft lip repair is a basic and common surgery, and it would make a huge difference in his life going forward. I would need to consult with our board, but I was confident we could help with the costs of this surgery. The weight of her crisis had suddenly just become lighter. "Really?" was her reply, as tears of relief rolled down her cheek.

We encouraged Arzu to borrow money for the surgery and to come to us with receipts afterwards. Asking those we serve to come to us for reimbursement after they pay removes the temptation to use the money for other expenses, since they often face multiple critical demands on their finances. Arzu returned a few months later. Her baby had healed well from the surgery; he was nursing well.

Fifteen months later Arzu came to us again with a different request. She wanted help with the costs of an abortion. She was fearful that another baby would be born with the same deformity. I assured her that such conditions are extremely rare. We could only trust God together. We offered her prenatal care and asked her to return in two months' time.

When Arzu returned two months later she informed us that she had lost the baby. We grieved, though she seemed relieved; the thought of another dependent was more than she could bear.

She and her husband have faced many other struggles during their years in Istanbul. On one visit she reported that her husband was arrested and sent to a detention center. Remarkably, his Turkish employer traveled to the detention camp to plead for his release because he had a wife and young children. We marveled and rejoiced at his care for the family. Because of his influence, Arzu's husband was released. More recently Arzu's oldest son broke his arm, and the father removed the cast himself because they did not have enough money for a follow-up appointment.

Arzu and her family will surely face more hardship. They do not belong here; they remain strangers in Istanbul. Yet they cannot go back to Afghanistan – their only way forward is to endure and to navigate each crisis as it comes. Like Arzu, countless families face crisis upon crisis. Our calling is to serve them wisely, faithfully, and generously, trusting that even small acts of care can bear the mark of God's mercy.

“What would you do if you were me?” Shahram stood close to me. I could see the intensity in his wide-open eyes, his eyebrows raised. I could hear the urgency of his voice, and from his pulsing veins I could sense his rapidly beating heart. Shahram was near panic. He had been given ten days to leave the country or be deported. Shahram, Iranian-born and now in his early 20s, was one of our translators. He had come to the program through an Iranian church, and he had a soft heart for the people we served.

It was late in the summer of 2015. Tens of thousands of refugees and migrants were crossing from Turkey to Greece. When Shahram, through his church community, had come to faith in God, his conscience was stirred. He had previously listened to bad advice from a relative in the UK and had lied about his age on his application for refugee status. Shahram had believed that his case would be stronger if he presented himself as an abandoned minor. Shahram had reported that he was 17 years old, that he had no family, and that he had been persecuted in Iran.

After waiting for over a year, Shahram was called for an interview. He was convinced that if he was honest about his age and admitted his lie, the officials would honor his integrity, make an exception, and grant him refugee status.

When the clerk heard his confession, she wrote "disqualified" across his file. She refused to listen to any other details. To her it was a clear case of deception; he was now marked as untrustworthy. Shahram pleaded with her, but he was dismissed from her office and told that he had 10 days to return to Iran or be deported.

"What would you do?" Shahram pressed me, though he had already decided what his next steps would be. He wanted his decision to be affirmed. I told him that I could not say what I would do. I am not in his situation. It is hard for me to even begin to imagine. It pains me that all his options are hard and risky, I told him. We gave him some supplies to help him on the journey, and I reassured him that we would pray for him and eagerly await news.

Shahram came to say goodbye to us and to collect his final pay. He planned to travel by land to Greece with a group of other migrants. He would have no phone or personal documents, hoping for a fresh start and a new identity when he arrived. He promised to be in touch. We gave him food and said goodbyes and began a hard few days of waiting and wondering.

Then one morning Shahram reappeared. His arms and legs were peppered with bites, the skin inflamed and raw from itching. We treated him with anti-itch cream and gave him some to take on his next journey. He would now join a group that would attempt to cross by boat. The land border had been a miserable, failed experience. Lying in marshland for three nights to avoid capture had been a nightmare. Shahram's experience was similar to reports from the early years of the program when migrants were caught on the border between Turkey and Greece, and many perished. Yet I can still see Shahram's smile. He had not lost hope, and he found strength in serving others making the same journey and knowing he was not alone.

A few weeks later I received a text message from a Greek cell number. Shahram was safe. He had found work on a Greek island, and a new chapter of his journey had begun. I have lost touch with Shahram, but I know that he will continue to serve others with generosity, just as he did with us.

Crises force choices no one should have to make – between truth and survival, integrity and safety, principle and the next meal. Those of us who care for people like Shahram feel the same strain in different ways, weighing rules against mercy, fairness against need. There are no easy answers, only the conviction that every person caught in crisis bears God's image and deserves to be met with grace and compassion.

Rivers of water flowed down our street, and floodwaters rose to two feet in our downtown area during an unusually dramatic rainstorm. My brother-in-law, John, was visiting and we had planned a special, one-day hearing clinic. John and I sloshed our way to the refugee center during the worst of the storm. We arrived soaked to find the courtyard outside my office flooded. We had the rare chance to offer life-altering care to children who had severe hearing impairment, but we feared the chance would be lost due to weather. It would take enormous commitment for families to make the journey to our center on a day like this.

Over the previous ten months, several refugee or migrant children had come to our center suffering from profound hearing loss. The cost for this kind of help was beyond our normal resources. I made a note in their records, hoping that somehow we might find a way to help. Knowing that John had expertise in this area, I mentioned the need to him.

For a number of years my sister Nancy and her husband John traveled to Romania to volunteer in a poor transient community. John has become skilled at fitting hearing aids. When John and Nancy heard of our need, they arranged to spend a few days with us on their way to Romania and to offer a one-day hearing clinic. We contacted the families, some of whom would have to travel two hours to reach us.

This was a chance for a consultation, we told them. We could offer no promises.

They all came. Clearly it was God who brought them! One young boy had been injured in an explosion in Afghanistan; he had journeyed overland from Afghanistan to Turkey with his mother and siblings the previous year. A piece of shrapnel had been removed from his ear, but he had also suffered abuse from his father because of his deafness. He had a bright beaming smile as John adjusted the settings for the hearing aids. He could hear! His mother was equally amazed.

Another mother called her son's name from across the room, and he turned at the sound of her voice. Behind her veil she reached with one hand to wipe tears from her eyes while her other hand covered her mouth. Her son had heard her voice for the first time.

That day reminded us how deeply these families value every chance given to them. Even a storm could not stop them; when opportunity was offered, they met it with a perseverance that still humbles me.

The tiny, premature baby boy was buried in a thick bundle of blankets. He looked fragile and pale, and he was quiet. Too quiet. Little Ali had just been released from three weeks in the ICU. Zeynab brought him, along with her hospital receipts, to ask for help with the cost. Her husband was working nights at a car wash. The family had been in Istanbul for three years. Ali was her third son, and Zeynab had received help from us with her first two pregnancies.

The bills that Zeynab showed us totaled far more than the family could ever imagine repaying. To someone from North America, $10,000 may seem a bargain price for three weeks in an ICU; for Zeynab the cost was astronomical, though the hospital had already reduced the bill by a third out of compassion.

Zeynab was grateful just to have her newborn with her. It had been a struggle to get him released to her care, and the hospital administrator had kept her passport as a guarantee of payment. She would be thankful for any help that we could give.

We talked with Zeynab about strategies to get back her passport. It was illegal for the hospital to seize her passport, but it was not uncommon. While we were talking, the baby made no sound. Zeynab had been unable to breastfeed him, and he was weak. She was producing some milk but told me that it was not enough. We coached her on breastfeeding, but I knew that nursing a premature baby is especially challenging.

Ali, the tiny newborn, seemed so fragile to me against the chaos and cruelty of the world he was born into. I remember when the hospital released our firstborn to our care. Her dependence and fragility felt overwhelming. How much harder for Zeynab! With all of the other challenges she faced, a quiet bundle in the corner could be easy to ignore. To breastfeed every two hours is a full-time job. Yet the God-given instinct to care for and nurture new life is remarkable, and Zeynab was motivated. She had been a good mother to her other two boys. Now the demands on her were much greater as she cared for a three-year-old, a one-year-old, and a fragile, premature son.

Zeynab's love for her children speaks eloquently. In her I see both the cost and the beauty of perseverance in the face of crisis – the same spirit we saw in Miriam's determination, in Arzu's endurance, and in Shahram's courage to begin again. Each person we encounter is a reminder that the God who watched over Mary far from home in Bethlehem and Hagar in the wilderness calls us to care for mothers like Zeynab who are raising children in exile and fear. Yet both those who serve and those who suffer face exhaustion. The challenge – for migrants and those who care for them – is to find sources of resilience.

Resilience

Come to me, all who labor and are heavy laden, and I will give you rest.

Matthew 11:28

It was July. The center was closed for a month. We boarded a flight from Istanbul to Toronto to visit family. Soon after our arrival, I would travel to a weekend conference on trauma and counseling. I had read books by the speakers, Ed Welch and Darby Strickland, and I thought highly of them. But was it realistic for me to attend? It felt like a stretch to add an extra flight and a conference to our already busy travel schedule, but I knew I needed to be better equipped to care well for both refugees and volunteers.

The talks on trauma and its effects on the body and the soul were all relevant to my work. Speakers at the conference talked a lot about "compassion fatigue." That resonated; I felt weary in soul and body. It was useful, not life-altering.

But one session stopped me short. In that session Ed Welch asked Darby Strickland, who counsels abused women, "How do you not get knocked down by the hard stories that you hear?" "Good question," I thought! Her response: "I try not to work with more than one very hard case at a time." When I heard that, tears came to my eyes. One hard case at a time! We saw as many hard cases as we had appointments in the day. We sometimes counseled 30 women and their families in a day, and we had no control over what stories they would bring to us, what crises were waiting at our gate. For sure, the stories of trauma and abuse were punctuated by humorous moments; we experienced intervals of joy. But the backstory of everyone we met with involved enduring pain and intense trauma. When the session ended, I approached the speakers to express my appreciation. Ed Welch asked me what kind of work I do. When I told him that I was working with refugees, my tears returned. Ed Welch did the only thing he could do for me at that moment: he stopped and prayed for our work and for the burden that I was carrying.

What I was experiencing is sometimes called secondary trauma. Those who care for the wounded come away with scars of their own. The challenge had been recognized from the program's earliest years. Though it seldom shows up in reports, volunteers faced daily heartbreak long before the term "compassion fatigue" became familiar. Almost every person who comes to us has suffered trauma, and many of them arrive at our gate still in the midst of crisis. Our volunteers take on the burden of their stories day after day, often feeling helpless and sometimes angry.

In refugee work such as ours, translators are especially vulnerable. Translation has been a necessary part of the program from the very beginning. Often the role is filled by those who themselves are refugees or migrants. They know the language and culture; they understand the refugee journey; they are aware of available resources. Translators can often discern when a story doesn't sound right, and they can offer advice about possible resources that they have encountered. But they also have painful stories of their own.

I was at my office door waiting for a client to come to my desk when I saw that our translator Leila had stepped away from the table where she had been registering a new client. This was not normal. I went over to see what was wrong. It was clear that she was disturbed. Someone else replaced her at the table to finish out the conversation, and the two of us walked to the back of the garden. She shared with me, through tears, that the story she was hearing had evoked painful memories of her own similar experiences from when she had been in detention. Vivid images tumbled into her mind. Sights, sounds, and smells of those weeks that she had spent alone in detention. It was too much. She needed space. We shed tears together. We prayed together. She went for a short walk and had a drink before resuming at another desk where the story was more familiar and predictable. Leila recovered. She adapted to that trauma and was able to see that God met her in it. She continues to serve years later.

Leila had lived out the instructions that I often gave to our whole team when we met at the start of a day: Step away from the table when you need to and take a break; change position to help reorient; change your breathing by standing up and walking; take time to look around at the world that we are in. We are blessed to serve in a garden, a place of relative calm in the middle of the city. The garden is a gift for us as a team, and for those whom we serve. We can look up at the green of the trees, watch the birds forage for crumbs that have been dropped, see the blue sky, or listen to the rain. We need these reprieves, even when brief.

Another volunteer, Megan, struggled with infertility. She longed for God to give her a child. We know this ache from stories in the Bible, and we often encountered it among the women who came to us. In some cultures, a woman's status is in question until she bears a child. One minute, we might be praying for a woman who was struggling with infertility; the next moment counselling with a young woman pleading for an abortion, unable to face the burden of another child. There was little we could do for either situation, except counsel and pray.

Megan needed to be cared for. She could be fragile with hope or raw with grief. The ache of infertility is often private, and I was honored that Megan shared her struggles with me. One day I checked in with her to be sure she would be okay registering the women newly coming to us who were pregnant, had new babies, or were being reimbursed for birth costs. The precious newborns wrapped in soft blankets would be celebrated and cuddled. They would also be a painful reminder of Megan's own unanswered prayers. Instead, Megan accepted my offer to switch desks, and she moved to registration and reimbursement for those with children in school.

Megan could make a choice to support her resilience; a refugee can't. A young mother of three small children, Nasim, came to the center weary with the burdens of displacement, poverty, motherhood, and illness. She was not coping with the stress. Her children were also suffering. Her oldest son, Husayn, was wetting the bed every night; her middle son, Ali, had outbursts of anger and was often out of control; her infant was not gaining weight with nursing. We began by trying to patiently address each issue with strategies and compassion. Nasim softened. She admitted, sheepishly, that she too struggled with outbursts of anger. She did not know how to cope in any other way. Shouting at her children had become a regular pattern. Nasim expressed shame, but also relief that someone cared to listen. Rather than just continuing to discuss strategies, Kara walked her to the back of the garden while another volunteer held her baby and supervised her other children. Kara demonstrated some breathing exercises and suggested ways to step away from a stressful situation. Kara pointed out the importance of seeing beauty. She told Nasim that this was one way to care for herself each day. "Keep the children safe," Kara said, "And step away, even if for less than a minute." The care that Kara showed Nasim was an imitation of our caring God. Nasim's posture and countenance were different when she headed home with the children that afternoon. She was encouraged and equipped in her own journey of resilience. The stressors would not be gone but she could carry them differently.

Engaging creativity is another way to build resilience. Trauma therapy often includes the creative arts. Over the years our volunteers have found many ways to engage those who come to us in art, movement, music and creativity. I loved to step out of my office and just observe what was going on. One day a paper chain stretched the length of the garden, attached to trees and supported by chairs while it blew in the wind, growing longer and more grand in the hands of the excited children. The rain and wind blew it away, but the process had been an unexpected joy. During another season, a vibrant forty-foot mosaic began to appear piece by piece, transforming a gray, concrete wall. With skillful coaching from one of our artist volunteers and the eager participation of some of the refugees and volunteers, the mosaic continued to slowly develop over four years.

Another volunteer, Terry, bought plants for our visitors to plant in the garden beds. For some of them it had been years since they had dug in the ground. One day I came out of the office to squeals of delight as Terry hosed down laughing children and women. Another day I stepped out to see a group of children cheering on snails as they inched across a wet surface on a rainy day.

Chocolate can also help. The Ecumenical Patriarch, Bartholomew, visited our program one day near Christmas, bringing a large, attractive box of chocolates for each mother, each child, and each volunteer. The children were thrilled and had chocolate on their hands very quickly as they tore into their gifts; the mothers were equally pleased by the colorful boxes. Probably not the moment to instruct on the need to avoid sugar when your body is stressed!

Zahra's smile is fixed in my mind. But when I saw that she had requested an appointment, I was hesitant to call her in. This was a new dilemma for us after the pandemic. For 29 years our gates had been open. Each Monday,

Wednesday, and Thursday people had lined up, sometimes hours ahead, to receive a number for their turn to be served. The pandemic had forced us to move to an online appointment system. It was more orderly; the beginning of our day was less chaotic. But it made us face difficult decisions, and I felt the loss of face-to-face interaction and the opportunity to do a quick triage. Reading from a list on paper was not the same.

I remember feeling torn when I saw Zahra's name. I knew her story. We had served her repeatedly. Should we call her in or give priority to those who had arrived more recently and might have more urgent needs? Something niggled in my heart and mind, "Could something be wrong? Has her situation changed?" I made her an appointment.

Zahra was a tall Afghan woman with a beautiful smile and warm eyes. In spite of her circumstances, she exuded joy. When Zahra first came to us on a winter day, she carried the documentation of her own refugee status and that of her third child, a handicapped daughter. Her husband and her other three children had documents but not refugee status. Zahra had a light wrap on against the biting cold. Her four children wore layers but not enough to stay warm. We provided coats to each of them from an emergency supply. The coats were bright Crayola colors. From her wheelchair, Zahra's young daughter screeched with delight.

I immediately saw that Zahra was a good fit for our partner Moms and Tots program. When I suggested it she was enthusiastic, and undeterred by the climb up five flights of stairs required to participate. Zahra loved the morning program. She listened eagerly to stories of Jesus. Her heart melted as she realized God's care for her, and his expression of his love through others. When she came to our office, she openly shared what she was thinking. We at the center continued to serve Zahra with food coupons and medical assessments. When her children entered school, we enrolled her in our education assistance program.

When I saw Zahra's name on the request list I was puzzled. She was no longer eligible for our programs; there was little more that we could offer her. But I was curious to know if there was something new in her situation. When she came, we quickly learned that her husband needed surgery for a wounded hand. Since their arrival in Turkey, he had worked long hours on the street collecting recycling materials from trash bins. It is difficult, dangerous work. Zahra reported that she and her husband were fighting more and facing severe financial stress. We probed more. The children were safe. Zahra had been hit, but not frequently. She saw it as coming from his pain and desperation. She genuinely seemed to care for her husband and did not seem to be covering for a long-time abuser. She wanted to do what she could to help. We gave her some financial help and asked her to come back in a month.

The following month Zahra's spirits were much brighter. Her husband had the surgery with the help of UNHCR connections. She was grateful for our help in their time of need.

She and her family remain in Istanbul, and this will likely be home for Zahra and her family for years to come. Like Zahra, many refugees who receive the UNHCR refugee designation will not be resettled to a third country. Only 1% of all refugees – one in a hundred – are resettled at the best of times. A refugee designation gives permission to remain in Turkey without fear of deportation, but it does little to make life sustainable. Much of our task, shared by our partner programs, is to come alongside such families and to help them weather crises and build resilience for the long haul.

Crises will come. By nature, they are unexpected. Resiliency describes our capacity to recover our footing, to adapt, and to move forward. How can we foster resilience?

Through long years of service, I have thanked God daily for my beloved family and friends who strengthen me. I've thanked him for the beauty of my ferry commute – watching for dolphins, breathing sea air, finding joy in small mercies. I've stepped away to see beauty, eaten too much chocolate, laughed, and prayed for sleep.

But my lifeline has been God himself meeting me in the pages of his Word. Reflecting on the life of Jesus – the weariness he felt, the crowds he pitied, the times he withdrew to pray – has anchored me. On mornings when I wondered how I could face the day, I cried out with the psalmist: "I lift up my eyes to the hills. From where does my help come? My help comes from the Lord, who made heaven and earth" (Psalm 121:1–2). He is my keeper, my shade at my right hand. In the Psalms, God's people pour out every emotion – joy, sorrow, anger, repentance – and always find him faithful. He is our refuge and strength. He is steadfast, immovable, just, and full of love towards us.

But in some situations, the strategies I have described in this chapter can seem almost trite. Stepping away, breathing deeply, creating beauty – none of it feels like enough. There are moments when even prayer seems beyond our reach. How do we face those times when the same garden that shelters laughter and healing also bears witness to stories of cruelty, domination, and violence?

Violence

The LORD works righteousness and justice for all who are oppressed.

Psalm 103:6

The Spirit of the Lord God is upon me, because the Lord has anointed me to bring good news to the poor; he has sent me to bind up the brokenhearted, to proclaim liberty to the captives, and the opening of the prison to those who are bound.

Isaiah 61:1-2, Luke 4:16-21

"Sunglasses don't make sense on cloudy days," I thought as I approached our locked gate. The woman at the front of the line in the narrow passage was wearing large sunglasses. She was young and tall. She appeared to be Afghan. I did not recognize her. Women had gathered there over the past 45 minutes and were now vying for a spot at the head of the queue to receive a number to be seen at a triage desk. Some had come for a prearranged appointment at the hospital; they would be taken by one of our translators to our partner hospital and we would pay for the costs of the day's tests and treatments. Others came to be checked by a nurse for their prenatal progress. Most had no appointment. For many years we were the only refugee program in Istanbul that accepted walk-ins. Sometimes I arrived to a line of more than 50 women. Determining who we could serve became more challenging over time. The crowds grew with new challenges.

This woman with sunglasses was named Mina. At her registration interview Mina did not remove her sunglasses. Julie, who registered her, was astute and knew this was an unusual situation. She came inside and asked for Mina to be interviewed privately. Julie mentioned the sunglasses. Right away I said, "Yes, by all means! Call her in." We pulled a curtain across so that we could speak in private, and I asked Mina to remove her glasses. When she did, I was stunned. She had two black eyes with large, round bruises the shape of a fist. I felt sick. She denied that she had been hit; she said she had fallen. I assured her that she was safe with us. I explained to her that the way God makes our eyes, surrounded by bones, makes it unlikely that a fall will leave bruises like this. But she continued to deny that she had been hit, and we could not press the point. I stressed that she was welcome to come back anytime for a hot meal, to join our exercise or art programs, or to find people to talk to and pray with. We made a note in her file and put a star on her ID card to indicate that she was to be considered vulnerable and should be admitted whenever she came.

Three weeks later Mina returned to us. This time she had bruises on her legs. "Yes," she said, "Sometimes my husband gets upset with me." We assured her that she is not alone and that her husband needs help. "This is not how God intends for us to be treated," I said. We asked about her son's safety. She said that he was fine; her husband had never hit him.

The family was under intense pressure. They were new to the city and undocumented. Her husband Ahmed had been working for a time, but he had been laid off. He wanted Mina to find work. Ahmed would stay with their son, he told her. Extended family members who were also in Istanbul did not know about the abuse, Mina told us. "Please don't tell anyone," she pleaded.

Cases like Mina's were among the most difficult that I faced. Early coordinators reported similar challenges, and Mina's story stands in a long line of such encounters. Under the second coordinator, the center began addressing gender-based violence among new arrivals. Reports from 1996 recorded growing numbers of women "arriving at the gate bearing bruises and shame, fearful that they will not be believed." Such encounters left me feeling powerless, helpless, angry, and sad. The stories of abuse lingered with me and would show up in my dreams. I would wake in the night crying. My prayers for the women were, "Lord, help! Lord, have mercy! Lord how long? Lord, protect!" There often seemed so little we could do.

A few weeks later Mina came to the gate late in the morning. We gave out numbers early and often had to turn people away. Latecomers were usually sent away. But this was different. Our gatekeeper saw panic and fear on her face. He interrupted me during an interview with another client. "Yes," I said, "absolutely have her come in and bring her straight inside." We asked others to leave the office to enable a private consultation.

Mina cried in pain. She needed help. She was unable to sit down. She showed me fresh wounds on her legs and back. The image is still seared in my memory. Her husband had beaten her with an electric cord. I wept with her. I gently held her, avoiding areas of open wounds. "We can help you," I told her, "But it is your decision."

It can be costly for any woman to leave an abusive husband. How much more for a vulnerable refugee woman in an unfamiliar city. Protection is available, but the woman must decide.

Mina said she wanted help. We made an emergency call to a partner organization that gives legal advice to refugees. They immediately sent counselors to our office.

They interviewed Mina, assessed her vulnerability, and with her permission placed her in a safe house. Mina left our garden facing the dangers and uncertainties of a costly decision.

For many days I thought about Mina and prayed for her. I knew that though we did not know the end of the story God knew. He knew where she was and what was transpiring. A month later Mina came to the gate beaming. The image of her smiling face at the gate is also imprinted in my mind. Her smile was broad. Her eyes sparkled. We were thrilled to see her. We learned the next chapter in her story, and it was rewarding.

The counselors had helped her to communicate with the police and the legal system. Her husband was arrested and detained overnight. Her two-year-old son was brought to her in the safe house. Mina stayed at the safe house for three weeks and then returned home to her husband. She knew that she could go to the police should an episode of violence occur. The police told her husband that he would be immediately deported if he abuses her. Many women in such a situation lose their nerve, change their minds. Sometimes authorities do not respond with this level of justice and compassion.

Mina spent that entire day with us. She had a hot meal. She participated in our art program. She listened to the Bible stories, and our volunteers prayed with her. "This is the place where I learned that I didn't have to endure being beaten," she said. As I remember, I am filled with gratitude to God for a safe place of refuge, for our compassionate volunteers, for all the love that Mina received.

I am also filled with gratitude for partnerships. Partnership is critical to working with the vulnerable. No organization can do it alone. Our office has been in the same place for all these years, and it developed partnerships right from the beginning. Assisting with legal concerns for refugees and migrants was a primary focus in the early years. The police have known who we are and where we are; they have sometimes brought vulnerable people to our door. At other times people arrived at our gate with a note scribbled on paper and a name or organization attached to it. We would honor those referrals to keep the lines of partnership open and to be able to refer in return when needed.

Domestic violence is a global issue. There are many who work tirelessly for the prevention and education against this evil expression of anger and dominance. It has been encouraging in our years here in Istanbul to see public service ads on metro trains, ferries, and buses. The message encourages victims to seek help and it informs witnesses to violence against women about how they can respond and report it.

To hear the stories of women who are suffering from violence is a costly privilege. They need protection and safety. They also need to be heard, valued, and loved. To victims of violence who come to us, I give the same assurance Hagar received from God. You are seen. You are loved. You have worth. There is a God who knows you, and he sees you. He is fully trustworthy, and he longs for you to know him. God made himself known to a woman, Hagar, who was in your circumstances. She was cast out to the desert to die and God called out to her. He provided for her and promised to care for her.

Abida always looked sad. She came to the center before I began volunteering. She can smile. I have seen it. But it takes work to coax a smile from her.

Abida journeyed with her husband from Afghanistan to Turkey more than a decade ago. Borders were easier to navigate then. Abida heard about our program from an Afghan friend. She had young children, and her friend knew that we provided young families with support for a good diet, health assessment, and education. Abida cannot read or write. Her sewing skills are minimal. Her husband worked in textile factories. When pressure mounts and debts accumulate, he becomes violent towards Abida. Both feel shame. Abida does not want to expose her husband; and in less stressful times, her husband expresses remorse and a desire to change. But neither knew where to turn for help.

Abida's husband has never come to the center. I have never met him. What I know about him I know through her reports. She sometimes talked about "troubles." She reports that he is diabetic and has other illnesses that have made his work hard on his body. When I asked Abida about her safety or the safety of the children, she never expresses a desire to leave. She says that her children are safe.

We referred Abida to a counselor through Doctors Without Borders. Unfortunately, she did not keep her appointments. Her case with their office was closed.

Abida takes great pride and joy in her children. She has birthed four children in Turkey. They are all attending school. The family has struggled hard to remain documented, paying the necessary fees each year to retain guest documents. Abida has been in the Moms and Tots program over the years. The volunteers there have also spoken into the need for the cycle of violence to stop.

But we have to give Abida autonomy in the decisions she makes. She has been offered help. She does not want to leave her husband. If she did, what future would she have? Could Abida remain here without him? We continue to give her the message of love and worth. Abida knows that when she comes to the center she will be heard, she will be cared for, and she will be assisted and prayed for. Abida knows that all of what we do is because we love God and want to express his love to her.

Domestic violence stories hit me hard, eliciting both deep sadness and anger. Domestic violence hides behind closed doors. It keeps its victims in bondage. It has no place in God's design. But we live in a broken and groaning world. The shame needs to be interrupted with the overwhelming love of God in Christ. Both parties need the message of God's deep care for them and his ability to help them to change.

There were some nights when I woke with vivid nightmares of the stories that I had heard. God provided wise counsel. A friend said, "Carol, you need to step away, even for a short period of time. You cannot ignore these signs of secondary trauma. Don't just push through."

We followed her advice and took some time away to rest, to be in sunshine, to walk, and to drive. It was a gift. But I felt guilty. I could step away and enjoy the beauty of the world; the woman whose life story had been keeping me awake at night could not. My tears came. Some of the tears were sorrow; others came from the overwhelming sense of injustice in our world, and still others from anger at the perpetrators of such evil. I asked God the questions that tumble out in moments of lament: How long, Lord? Why? What can be done?

One day we drove along a coastal road. I was in the passenger seat, absorbing the beauty of the turquoise sea glistening beside us. I said to Dan, “I wish I could sit and hear from God on these things.” The road had been deserted for miles. We had seen no people, no houses, no stores, no cars. The only sign of human presence in the area was the paved road. Then, suddenly, there was a clearing ahead. And in the clearing, on a patch of grass facing the glittering sea, I saw two empty chairs. I was stunned. “Dan!” I said, shocked, “Stop the car! Look!” God had answered me. He wanted me to sit with him. I photographed the scene so that I would never forget the surprise visitation. The photo wasn’t necessary; the image is deeply etched in my mind, a sign of the kindness of God to me in my journey with him.

A young Afghan woman sat down in the chair beside my desk. She had been in the garden for two hours waiting her turn to see a nurse. As we talked, she nursed her beautiful three-month-old daughter. Our examining room is tiny and busy, with two desks, a fan, tired furniture hidden with slip covers, and numerous volunteers constantly in and out. “How can I help you?” I asked. I often have little idea of what a patient wants to be seen for before they come. Back pain. Skin disorders. Chronic or acute issues. All have bodies that are exhibiting stress. "My finger hurts, and something is not right with it," she replied. I could see that her finger was deformed and not functional. She was in pain. "How and when did you injure your finger?" With each of my questions, a little more of her story came out.

Slowly, reluctantly the words came, and tears dropped down her cheeks. She had a much deeper wound she was wanting to share, but she was not sure either how to say what was on her heart or how much to reveal. Our eyes were fixed and my tears mirrored hers as she shared, and I listened. She is just twenty-two, far from home, with a three-year-old and a three-month-old, and she is a victim of domestic violence. We were able to splint her finger, and touch on her deeper wounds, to pray with her, and to point her towards help – for her safety and for her husband's need to change. But will she be able to take the next step? Often we have no idea.

Reading in the gospels, I notice that we are often given no more than a brief glimpse into the lives of those whom Jesus met. We meet the lame man or the blind man for a moment, and we can picture them. We can imagine Nicodemus during his secret, nighttime conversation with Jesus. And we hear that later he participated in the care of Jesus' dead body. But we aren't told the whole story. That story belongs only to the lame man, the blind man, Nicodemus, and God. We here are similarly left with momentary, often poignant encounters. We may learn a small part of the backstories. But for us the stories remain unfinished; we almost never know the end.

. . . people who speak thus make it clear that they are seeking a homeland . . . they desire a better country, that is, a heavenly one. Therefore, God is not ashamed to be called their God, for he has prepared for them a city.

Hebrews 11:13–16

Miriam carried the hopes of her entire extended family to Istanbul. They had sacrificed to purchase a passport and an airline ticket. She dreamed of sending money back, of helping to lift her family out of poverty. She quickly learned that the promises made to her were empty, the path of opportunity portrayed to her a staged background. She arrived to the realities of modern slavery; she had fallen into the hands of a ring of evil people. Miriam's passport was taken, and she was expected to participate in the sex trade. She was repulsed. With the courage of conviction and the strength of youth, she escaped.

Miriam found a safe place to live and search out work. But life was hard. She could barely make ends meet. She dared not communicate to her family the struggles she endured. At her workplace, Miriam met a kind man, also African. He cared for her and wooed her into a relationship. She became pregnant; he was not happy. Then she learned the devastating news that the baby might have Down Syndrome. Four months pregnant, burdened by this weighty anxiety, she was abandoned by the child's father when she refused to consider an abortion. A woman in her workplace saw her agony and told her about our center.

"You can help me, can't you?" Miriam pleaded. She was looking for rescue. "Yes, we can help you!" I replied. "But maybe you will not be eager for some of the possible ways." The best path that I could foresee for her was to go home to her family. She would need support, community, and belonging; in Istanbul she had few of these. I told her to think about it. But Miriam feared rejection by her mother. She could not imagine telling her mother that she was pregnant. And how could she bring a disabled child home to Uganda placing an additional burden on her extended family. She expressed shame and fear.

I shared with Miriam the Bible story of the Father waiting for his son to return from afar. His rebellious son had squandered his inheritance. But when he came to his senses, he knew that his best choice was to go home, hoping that his father might allow him to be a servant in the household. The beautiful surprise in the story comes when his Father, who has been watching for his return, runs to him while he is still on the road and embraces him with lavish, unbounded love.

I prayed with Miriam. I told her, as a mother, that we can handle more than our children give us credit for! Maybe her mother would react poorly on hearing hard news, but she would never stop loving her own daughter. Of course, cultures differ, but the love of a parent for their child is a deep human bond. The decision would have to be Miriam's. If she chose to not to return, we would help her with her prenatal care here in Istanbul and the costs of delivery. If she chose to go back, the window of time for her to return to Uganda would be limited. She would be unable to travel in the final months of pregnancy. When Miriam left the center that day, she had received a shared warm meal, grocery money, an upcoming medical appointment, prayer, and a lot to think about.

To remain in Istanbul as a single mother is a choice that many other women have made. They have a difficult life. They find ways to support each other. They are creative in the ways that they find work doing cooking or handicrafts, or providing childcare for others who have more regular work. But when they come to us in crisis, we often offer them the option of returning home.

Over the next few weeks, the idea of talking to her mom seemed more possible to Miriam. She missed her mom. They had a call, the miles melted away, and Miriam's heart was drawn home. We referred her to our friends at the IOM. The IOM would provide Miriam with plane tickets, travel documents, and a small startup allowance so that she would not arrive empty-handed. They would also help with her delivery costs in Uganda.

Weeks after her departure from Istanbul, Miriam sent me photos of her beautiful, healthy baby boy! The test indicating possible Down Syndrome had been wrong. Miriam was surrounded by family; her face was beaming. The dark clouds of the past months and years had passed. Her future would have many more hard moments as a single mom, but she was in a much better place to begin that journey, surrounded by family.

During the past thirteen years, as Dan and I have traveled from Istanbul to the United States or to Canada, we often notice other passengers carrying blue and white bags marked with the International Organization of Migration (IOM) logo. They sometimes have carry-on bags with the same blue and white marking. When I see them, my heart beats faster, I smile, and my eyes fill with tears. Many of these have had to flee their original home, but the IOM is helping them to find a new one. Others, like Miriam, are returning to family. They are the fortunate ones. Ahead of them lie new opportunities, new chapters, a future place to call home.

But each traveler carries more than luggage. They carry their story – their losses, fears, and hopes for what lies ahead. I wonder where they will settle, how they will be received, whether the new land will ever feel like home. I have heard those same questions in my office from refugees preparing for resettlement: excitement and fear mingled with anticipation, anxiety, and gratitude, all written on their faces.

The IOM was founded in 1951, originally to assist in resettling people displaced in Europe after World War II. Its predecessor committees were conceived of as temporary, but the IOM has evolved rather than be disbanded. More than 70 years later, the IOM is a key intergovernmental agency and today coordinates the United Nations Network on Migration. Over the past decade the number of forcibly displaced people around the globe – refugees plus internally displaced persons – has doubled, rising from around 60 million to over 120 million. Some are displaced by natural disasters – floods, earthquakes, famine. Others by human-made crises – conflict, war, genocide. The IOM's mission remains to ensure that migration is humane and orderly and that it benefits both migrants and the societies to which they move.

The IOM was one of the few refugee organizations that were present in Istanbul when our church-based program began. They have remained one of our most significant partners in serving the vulnerable, coordinating both resettlement and repatriation programs. One of the most common, recurring themes in coordinators' reports through the years has been the challenges of repatriation and coordination with the IOM.

Oliver came to Istanbul twelve years ago, an economic migrant from Nigeria, full of hope, with dreams of attending university and assisting his family back home. Oliver is one of hundreds of thousands of economic migrants in Turkey who come here looking for education, work, and opportunities for advancement unavailable at home. Many of them do well. Many others struggle. After two years in Turkey, Oliver brought his fiancé, Mary, from Nigeria and they were married. Mary, now his wife, was introduced to our programs when she was pregnant with their first child. She had two more pregnancies in their years together. We lost touch with Mary. She lived far out of the city center, and her situation was stable.

Through the Moms and Tots program we learned the shocking news that Mary had died. Suddenly the family was in crisis, and they desperately needed help. The details were fuzzy, but it seemed Mary had undiagnosed, untreated cancer that ravaged her body during a recent pregnancy. Following the birth, Mary declined rapidly and died in the hospital. The baby was now three months old, and Oliver was devastated, alone, and ill-equipped to face the challenges ahead. Grief paralyzed him. He seemed incapable of caring for himself or for his three children. Friends rallied around him and cared for the children for days at a time. We gave special financial support to some of the women who were helping the family. Then we learned that Oliver's water was cut off due to unpaid bills. Pride, shame, and grief all kept him from asking for help or knowing where to turn. Fear that he would lose his children also kept him isolated.

Brenda, a friend of Mary, pleaded with us to help. I told Brenda that we would help Oliver at any time. Her plan was to bring Oliver and the children to the center herself. But two months went by and Oliver never came. We tried to call him, but he did not answer his phone. I told our gatekeeper that if he saw an African man with three children at our gate, he was to immediately let me know. We would receive them whenever they arrived.

The program was winding down late one afternoon when Emre's keen eyes spotted a disoriented and fearful-looking African man with an infant and two older children clinging to him. Emre immediately crossed the crowded street and shepherded him into our garden.

Oliver was afraid and overwhelmed. We listed the ways we could help, including the option of returning home to family. In the months that we had been waiting for Oliver, I had reached out to an IOM case worker who was ready to expedite their case. If Oliver was willing, we could move forward quickly. The situation seemed dire. The children might be taken by the Turkish authorities due to apparent neglect. The best option was repatriation. While the two older children played on the swing set, we initiated a video call with IOM. The IOM staff patiently explained to Oliver the many steps still needed to make this happen.

Mary's grieving parents were eager to have their three grandchildren back home in Nigeria where they could be loved and cared for. The IOM receiving office in Nigeria interviewed them and determined that their home was a safe and suitable place for the family. Travel documents needed to be arranged, tickets and passports obtained. There were many steps in this process, yet Oliver was fragile, and their home was no longer fit to live in. The IOM staff later told me that this was the most difficult case they had been involved in over their decades of work. I could agree. Many steps required Oliver's involvement, but he often missed appointments. It seemed impossible.

One day Oliver showed up unexpectedly. I immediately called the IOM case worker. "Keep him there," she told me. "We are on our way." Some of the questions were beyond Oliver's ability to comprehend. "Do you want 500 euros in cash," they asked him, "or 1500 euros in kind?" Ten years of struggling to survive in Turkey and provide for his family and the recent trauma of Mary's death left him incapable of understanding such a question. Somehow we got through the interview.

Mary's friends, volunteers from Moms and Tots, our gatekeeper, our volunteers, and the IOM staff all came together to care for Oliver at a time when he was incapable of caring for himself. With their help, Oliver and his three children arrived safely home in Nigeria to grandma and grandpa. "What is a grandma?" the children had asked, unaware that they even had extended family. The people who worked to help this struggling family, and the depth of the care they showed, were part of an extraordinary team effort.

"Alicia can be admitted at any time," I told our gatekeeper. "You can interrupt me and bring her directly to my office." Though I've mentioned several such situations, these kind of instructions to our volunteers were unusual. Alicia's case was exceptional.

Alicia was referred to us by a Catholic parish priest. He called me to briefly tell me the details. Alicia was Filipino. She had recently been released after seven years in a Turkish prison serving a sentence for attempted murder. After her release, she was employed as a cleaner for the municipality and allowed to sleep on a cot in the basement of a municipality building. For the next six months she would be required to sign-in with the police four times each week. The police office to which she was required to report was on the opposite side of the city.

I didn't know if Alicia would show up. Sometimes the most vulnerable referrals never come. But Alicia did arrive at our gate, tired and nervous, carrying a handwritten note from her priest asking us to care for her on his behalf. Alicia had met the priest on his prison visits. He had delivered monthly care packages, including hygiene products and treats. While in prison Alicia suffered a heart attack and had a pacemaker implanted. She was prescribed several cardiac medications and needed her prescriptions renewed. We were able to assess Alicia and refer her to a cardiologist who would renew her prescriptions.

Over time as she felt more at ease, I pieced together more of Alicia's story. She had been a domestic worker for a Turkish family. Her employer came to her when she was alone in the kitchen and attempted to rape her. In self-defense, she took out a knife and told him to get away. He reported to the police that she had attempted to stab him and accused her of attempted murder. She had no witnesses, no status, and her court-appointed lawyer failed to adequately defend her. Alicia was convicted and sentenced to seven years in prison.

As we counseled Alicia, we asked questions about her future. Could she return to the Philippines? Alicia was unsure. Her son, now an adult, was no longer there. Her family had disowned her after she was convicted and imprisoned. She had been shunned by the Filipino community in Istanbul. She was truly alone. We suggested that the church might provide an open door to receive her. Gradually over the course of her visits to our office, Alicia warmed to the idea.

Months went by, and we did not hear from Alicia. She had no phone. All we could do was pray. Then, one spring morning when I arrived at our gate, I was surprised to find Alicia waiting. I invited her into our office and learned that she had been sent to Erzurum in eastern Turkey, for further mandatory service at a government office there. While there she had been ill and had run out of heart medications.

I told Alicia that it was urgent that she make plans to leave Turkey. But she had no passport, and our conversation evoked another painful experience. Her passport had been seized by her abusive employer. He had married her off, on paper, to his driver to make it legal for Alicia to stay in Turkey. The marriage was not real, and after her employer got her Turkish citizenship, he lowered her wages and refused to pay into her social insurance account. Each chapter of Alicia's story uncovered more pain and injustice.

Because Alicia had Turkish citizenship, the IOM, which handles repatriation cases, was barred from helping her; only foreign nationals could qualify for repatriation. We set out to help Alicia obtain a passport, and we told her that we would pay for a one-way ticket to Manila using special donations. Representatives of the Catholic Church in Manila were prepared to receive her and to help her with resettlement. Time was short because a holiday was approaching.

But Alicia never returned. My eyes tear up and a spontaneous prayer of lament wells up as I recall her story and the deep injustice that seems unanswered: "Lord, I told Alicia that justice will be done in the end. I told her that you feel the pain of the oppressed. Let justice roll down. May those who are evil meet their judge and your day of reckoning come for the oppressors."

I often watched for Alicia. I would look twice when I saw a Filipina woman of her age and stature. I never learned what happened.

Leyla, age thirteen, returned to Afghanistan. She had left her country of birth and citizenship with her parents when she was only four years of age. She had no memories of the "home" that she returned to. She returned to people she did not remember, to an extended family she did not know.

Leyla has deep brown eyes and dark hair. Her smile is bright. She is curious. She loves to doodle. In a Turkish public school, where classes sometimes have 40 students, Leyla had learned to read and write and to make her presence known. Leyla's teachers had told her mother, Behnaz, that her daughter was smart. But when her mother developed cancer and began the difficult process of treatment, Leyla began to miss school and fall behind. Behnaz would not leave her beautiful daughter alone at home for hours after school while she was in treatment. They stayed together, an inseparable pair.

Leyla's father had left Turkey for Europe and disappeared from their lives. Behnaz and Leyla were forced to learn how to make their way together. Behnaz had a strong drive to get Leyla to Europe. The opening seemed to come in the winter of 2020. Rumors spread that the border to Greece was open. Along with hundreds of other refugees, Behnaz and Leyla traveled by bus to Turkey's western border. Behnaz hid their passports and residence permits in her bra. They took only one small bag with other precious possessions and joined a small group to cross the border into Greece. As they approached the river that marked the border, four men put Leyla onto a makeshift raft while Behnaz and the others in their group waded into the frigid, deep water.

On the other side, they were met by Greek police. All of their possessions were taken from them, and they were forced to retrace their steps back into Turkey. Behnaz's money and gold jewelry were stolen from her. Somehow, she managed to keep her residence card. What she didn't know was that the dangerous and terrifying journey had also led to the cancellation of her residence permit by the Turkish authorities. She had failed to make a required visit to an immigration office at the far east end of Istanbul to have her residence permission reviewed.

A year later when Leyla was not admitted to school because of a cancelled residence permit, Behnaz, struggling with cancer, went to the office of immigration to fight for permission for Leyla to be able to return to school. Instead of finding compassion or help, Behnaz and Leyla were both sent to prison. A prison doctor advocated for Behnaz. He realized that Behnaz did not have her oral chemotherapy drugs with her, and he insisted to the authorities that Behnaz and Leyla be released. Leyla, only eleven years old then, had spent a week in a Turkish prison cell with her sick mother.

Leyla's childhood was a story of pain, loss, and trauma but also opportunity. Utilities worked; a good public transport was part of her life; her mother demonstrated strength, advocacy and determination; Leyla thrived at school; and her Turkish was better than her Dari.

But illness was taking her mom from her. If Behnaz died, Leyla would become a ward of the state. We could see that Behnaz had only a short time to live, but Behnaz was unable to face her mortality.

When we gently approached the topic of her prognosis, she insisted that she would be with Leyla. This made it impossible to help her plan for Leyla's future in Turkey after she was gone. We had conversations with lawyers at Refugee Rights Turkey and learned that if Behnaz would sign documents, then Leyla could be guaranteed schooling and housing through her university years. We never had those conversations with Behnaz, as her own death remained inconceivable to her.

Behnaz decided that her best course was to return to Afghanistan. Leyla returned as a stranger to her passport country. Leyla would be a female dependent in a world where women are excluded from public life. She is a Turkish-educated young woman now denied access to further education. Afghan girls like Leyla are frequently married off young, sometimes as second wives to older men. Though difficult, life in Turkey had been vibrant and given her opportunity and freedom. Now she is in a place where those opportunities are stripped from her. Leyla has become a reverse migrant, returned to a "home" that she never remembers as home.

I have often prayed for Leyla. I have asked God to protect her, and to reveal himself to her. I have prayed that she will recall the many times we had conversations and shared stories of the Bible. Behnaz had told Leyla that God is a God of love and that he would never leave her as an orphan; I had replied that, yes, God is a God of love and that in our broken world, he takes the side of the orphan, the widow, and the refugee. Jesus came to earth and lived among the vulnerable, the sick, the needy – he understands our suffering and meets us in it. I still pray that Leyla will come to see that same presence surrounding her, that the God who met Hagar in the wilderness and walked among the poor still walks beside her today.

For the displaced, for migrants, for exiles – even those who successfully adapt and work hard to make a life for themselves in a new place – the longing for home runs deep. The Scriptures give voice to that ache: "By the waters of Babylon, there we sat down and wept, when we remembered Zion" (Psalm 137:1). Far from home, the exiled Israelites remembered the temple and the songs once sung within its courts. They ached for return, and their sorrow became song – poems of lament born from the memory of belonging. That same ache runs through the stories of today's refugees and migrants.

I have felt the same ache. For more than 30 years I carried a much-sought-after "green card." The card, labelling me a "Resident Alien", became part of my identity, a critical document to be on my person whenever I crossed a border. It was also a constant reminder that I was an outsider; I did not belong. Once when I arrived in Boston, the border guard accused me of being an imposter because the photo on my alien card was so old. He tried to persuade me to surrender it. After that experience, I finally decided it was time to apply for US citizenship.

Why had I held out so long? Deep down I knew that I was Canadian. I belonged where I came from, where my history was, where my family lived.

My story does not involve trauma. Some people who flee are deeply grateful to be granted a new citizenship and a new passport, but they still carry a sense of home. We feel a loyalty to the people and places that have shaped us. A sense of place is implanted in us. I swore an oath of citizenship at a ceremony in Washington DC, together with seven other adults, citizens of Brazil, Colombia, Egypt, Mexico and the United Arab Emirates. Each of us pledged allegiance, but we didn't stop being proudly Brazilian, Colombian, Egyptian, Mexican, Arab – or Canadian.

After he returned home to Rwanda, Gaspard sent an email to the team of volunteers serving at the center. For 21 years Gaspard had been in our program, first as a recipient of services, then as a volunteer, and then as the assistant to the coordinator, serving under four different coordinators. A refugee himself, he faithfully and compassionately cared for other refugees and migrants. During his years with the center, Gaspard counseled thousands of migrants and refugees.

Gaspard adapted to Turkey. He was fluent in Turkish. But it never became home. As he grew older, he realized that there was no future for him in Istanbul, and he made the difficult decision to return home. His email poignantly expresses both the joys and challenge of return:

> For 11 days I went to the northwestern village areas, where I was born. It's a collection of nine small villages, where the Internet and electricity are absent. People are farmers with old methods… A couple of my old friends were still alive. But wounds of war were still fresh. In my own family we lost too many members of our family, and the neighbors from the other side also lost their beloved.
>
> In my area there is a wind of reconciliation. I visited and chatted with both sides… Many churches [of] different denominations are playing a major role in reconciliation. I was very happy to see some interethnic happy marriages.
>
> I visited my brothers and three of my four sisters. So many cousins, nephews… and so many half-brothers, uncles and aunties… I was happy to be able to meet them.
>
> Home is home, despite the old standard of life, these eleven days made me happy… At the end I met so many young people who are candidates to leave the villages because of hardship and hoping to change their lives. I told them some of what I know about going and living abroad and they can make their choices. They know now that it is a bittersweet experience.

Death

Teach us to number our days that we may get a heart of wisdom.

Psalm 90:12

"Gaspard is no longer with us." The words appeared on my phone while I was at my desk, with a client sitting across from me. I was shocked. My heart broke with the news. Not Gaspard! A few weeks before we had heard from Gaspard's nephew in Rwanda that Gaspard was ill with Covid-19. He was admitted to the hospital. Then news came that he was in the ICU. We sent funds to help with his mounting medical costs. Now he was gone.

Somehow it did not seem possible that Gaspard would not make it through this battle; he had overcome so many others. Life is fleeting, a vapor. But some people leave a lasting legacy of love and service that remains long after they are gone. Gaspard was one of those. I stepped out of the office and phoned one of our old volunteers. I wanted to talk to someone who knew and loved Gaspard and shared my grief.

"A joyful heart is good medicine." That verse from Proverbs captures Gaspard's personality. His smile was bright, his spirit warm and strong. In his youth, he had been selected to study at a university in Moscow. Three years later, en route to Rwanda to renew his passport and visit family, he became stranded in Istanbul. Though he intended to finish his studies in engineering in Russia, he was in transit in 1994 just as Rwanda descended into genocide. Between five hundred thousand and one million people, primarily Tutsi, as well as many moderate Hutu, were killed in about 100 days. Rwanda was in chaos. Gaspard's passport expired, and he became a man without a country. Return was impossible.

In Turkey the situation for African men was difficult. Gaspard experienced this firsthand. He decided that his best option was to seek a future in Europe. He planned to enter by land through Greece, avoiding border patrols. A young European couple convinced him they would protect him, and he traveled with them by bus. Tragically, they had no intention of protecting him but instead planned to use him to smuggle drugs across the border by placing their luggage with him as border controls searched the bags and passports. They went to the bathroom and reboarded the bus as Gaspard was taken by authorities. Many years later, when he told me the story his feelings of betrayal were still fresh. Gaspard was charged with possession of illegal drugs and sent back to Istanbul, convicted, and imprisoned. During his incarceration, Catholic fathers who visited him kept Gaspard's faith alive. Even when released, Gaspard experienced the horrors of being rounded up with other African men and shipped out to the east of the country to await deportation. He spent a terrifying night on a bridge in the cold of winter when as a group they were denied entry to Syria, Iraq or Turkey. Without documents they were men without a country.

Early coordinator reports document events like those Gaspard described. In the winter of 1992–93, several reports described a crisis involving African and Middle Eastern men who were rounded up in Istanbul and transported to Turkey's eastern frontier. Visitors to a detention camp in Silopi describe tent accommodation, inadequate clothing, and winter cold. In early records, both the first and second coordinator reported that "men without a country" continued to appear at the center office. Gaspard's ordeal on the bridge, therefore, stands not in isolation but as part of a grim pattern that marked the program's earliest advocacy work: confronting the inhumanity of border expulsions and affirming the worth of those caught, literally, between worlds.

Miraculously Gaspard made his way back to Istanbul and his street smarts served him well. All the while as the years had passed, his family in Rwanda had endured such unthinkable tragedies that their worlds grew farther and farther apart. Gaspard could not share his own story of sufferings, and they did not share with him. Gaspard could only imagine that his family resented him and thought that he had abandoned them, when in fact it was his deep desire to be with them.

A friend suggested that Gaspard come to the center for help. He recounted being warmly welcomed, joining the community meals and games as well as being offered wise counsel. He asked for help with resettlement, but his record of conviction made it impossible. The garden office became a home for Gaspard for the next decade and more. He had amazing language ability and became a valuable translator at the center. His own connections in various African communities made him an invaluable resource as volunteers met with migrants and refugees to listen to their stories.

When I began volunteering, Gaspard's warm smile and irrepressible spirit were among the most welcoming features of the program. But I had no idea of his backstory. His joy and compassion allowed him to serve the vulnerable despite his own pain, and his experience gave him empathy. Gaspard knew how and when to ask the follow-on question that would help to shed more light on a situation. He understood the weight of trauma, and though he had no formal training in trauma-informed counseling, he was a natural at caring for those in need.

Finally, in 2015, more than 20 years after he had been stranded in Istanbul, Gaspard decided that it was time to return home to Rwanda. He was nervous about how he would be received. With the help of IOM, Gaspard was able to get clearance for a one-way ticket to Rwanda. The board and volunteers of the center organized a special dinner and program to honor Gaspard. Many told stories of how he had impacted their life. With much love and many accolades from those he was leaving, Gaspard made the journey. He wrote later of how alone he felt on the plane. He journeyed to his village, and for days he sat with family members, listened to their stories, and grieved at their shared losses of family. It was a complex re-entry, but "Home is home" he had written to us.

Now he really was home.

Death, loss, and grief were not new to me. I grieved as an eight-year-old girl when Claudette, a friend my own age from church, died of leukemia. She was kind and gentle. Suddenly, she was gone. It was not easy to understand. As a ten-year-old, I learned that family friends had lost their month-old baby to crib death. It tore them apart. "Why would God take a baby?" I remember asking. As a teen, when I learned that my grandmother had died 3,000 miles away from where

I lived, I sat on my bedroom floor and wept. She had been a source of unconditional love, and now she was gone. I was with my grandfather when he died in his bed in my parents' home. I watched with my mother and brother as Grandpa's life faded and he strained to express his love with the few words he had left.

As a nurse, I have seen death come in many forms – sometimes lingering, sometimes sudden, shocking, and inconceivable. As a member of a hospice team, I cared for people and their families in the final days and weeks of life. Our goal was to bring comfort and support in this final season. We focused on helping the dying to live well, aware that their time was limited. For some, it meant rich weeks of family gathered and stories shared, with pain and death kept at bay. For others, it was a dark and lonely season filled with fear, with minimal support from absent family. End-of-life care is, as it states, care for the one dying and for all those witnessing the end. An especially weighty part of my work was being on call at night – leaving home in the dark to support a family in the final hours or to pronounce someone dead.

Grief was also the prelude to my work in Turkey. While we were preparing to leave, first for a year in Oxford, then moving to Istanbul, my father was in his final days of his life. Our family gathered around him. We shared memories.

We sang hymns. We prayed with him and told him we loved him. We were so thankful to be there when he took his final breath. Then he was gone. In the dark that night I remember suddenly sitting upright and struggling to breathe. The loss felt acute, and final. Dad had always been "in my corner." Now he was gone. This loss was of a different nature than previous losses.

I carried the loss with me to Oxford, and I experienced God's mercy there. The interlude gave me margin to grieve. I spent hours in the lovely beauty of Port Meadow. I took healing walks in the many parks of the city. But grief does not follow a predictable pattern. I was caught off guard when I turned a corner and saw a man on an electric scooter, just like my dad. It took my breath away. No, dad was gone. Grief is rather like an uncharted route on stormy seas, never the same twice.

When I have encountered grief and death in caring for refugees, I have sometimes been separated from them by miles. Those times provide no opportunity for closure, no opportunity to say goodbye. At other times I was left with silence, memories, and questions.

"Will you help me purchase a sewing machine?" Behnaz pleaded. This is Behnaz, mother of Leyla, whose story we have heard. It was the first time that I met Behnaz. Not often do women come to us with a realistic business plan. I was impressed. "Yes! We will! Today I will give you money for a sewing machine. In the fall you can return for school money for your daughter and tell me how things are going."

Months later Behnaz returned for the school money. As we chatted in the office, she shared with me that her left breast had been causing her pain. She felt a lump. I was alarmed. "Please use today's payment to see a doctor," I told her. She could return later for school money and to bring us the medical report.

Behnaz returned three weeks later, two days after a scheduled chemotherapy session. She had missed the appointment because she did not have enough money to pay the bill. The pathology report indicated stage four breast cancer. My heart sank. Behnaz was a single mom with an eleven-year-old daughter. This would be a major crisis for both.

I consulted with other volunteers and with our board. We decided to adopt her as a special case so that we could give her more than our normal medical assistance. This was the beginning of our long journey with Behnaz to care for her during cancer treatment. We would do what we could, but we never promised in such cases to be able to do it all.

As I witnessed Behnaz face multiple struggles, I came to admire her strength and determination. She was an amazing self-advocate. She knew how to ask for help, and sought out partnership wherever she could find it; nothing would deter her.

To better understand her treatment plan, I accompanied Behnaz to her doctor's appointments and to her chemotherapy treatments. Sitting across the desk from the oncologist, we were quite a pair. We were often asked, "How do you know each other?" Without hesitation, Behnaz would reply, "She is my mother." I did not contradict her, but I added, "We met through a church program to help refugees." Those we encountered were often as kind as they were curious. Knowing the nature of cancer, I was anxious for Behnaz to get beyond the chemo and to have surgery.

On chemotherapy days, I was prepared to run between departments to get various documents and approvals so that I could relieve Behnaz of the exhausting extra steps. This meant visiting several offices and waiting in line at each as well as going between buildings. When we had gathered all of the necessary documents, we sat together outside the chemotherapy unit, talking. Each time I learned more of her story. Behnaz was a remarkably determined young woman, and she never gave up hope for the future. She had entered Turkey legally seven years earlier along with her husband

and four-year-old daughter. Her husband was hired to work in Istanbul, and their airfare was paid. They were granted residence permits to live and work in Turkey. Behnaz worked at home and cared for her daughter. They had left behind family in Afghanistan, but their lives in Turkey were much better. Although they never considered returning home to Afghanistan, the couple did dream of going on to Europe.

In the summer of 2015, Behnaz's husband left her and his daughter behind and crossed to Greece with smugglers. He promised he would call for her. He did call once from a refugee camp, asking her to send money, so she knew he was alive. But many years later, she had no news of him. Behnaz moved on and adjusted to life as a single mother. She was fiercely proud that her daughter could read and write and was excelling in school.

Five chemo treatments at three- or four-week intervals gave us a lot of time together. I prayed with Behnaz, and for her, that God would grant her a long future with Leyla. I saw her strong and curious spirit exhibited in her interactions with others. I learned more of her story and the turning points in her life.

One dark snowy winter morning, I arrived at the hospital ahead of Behnaz. I had visited the ATM to get the cash she needed, and I obtained a number for her to see the doctor since the line was long. When Behnaz arrived, she had Leyla with her. My heart sank and my mind raced. The night before I had messaged her to say that I was not free to stay for the whole of her treatment. I told Behnaz that she would have to bring a friend or make a plan for Leyla. Suddenly my plans had to change. After getting Behnaz settled in the chemotherapy day center, Leyla and I headed out together.

I had very little with me in my backpack. What would we do for the day? I had called to change my plans of meeting someone at my office. Could I take Leyla there with me? I quickly dismissed this thought. Being on public transit with an undocumented young Afghan girl would not be wise.

We went to a nearby stationery store, bought a sketch pad, markers, and pencils, and settled for a long wait in a small restaurant close to the hospital. While snow swirled outside, we enjoyed soup and bread. On a napkin, I began to teach Leyla some simple paper and pencil games. The Turkish woman who had served us was curious. "How are you related?" she asked. I said that I was a friend of her mother, and that we were waiting together. We were an unlikely pair. The restaurant staff gave us limitless tea as morning turned into afternoon. Their kindness and hospitality are memorable.

In the weeks that followed, Behnaz's chemotherapy ended. New tests were done to determine if she was ready for surgery. Then, unexpectedly, Behnaz decided to seek advice and help elsewhere. I was stunned. Her Afghan friends had questioned the care she had been receiving and took her to another doctor. I was concerned and disappointed, but we had to honor her autonomy. She wanted us to continue to support her financially, but we could not give her money without knowing how she was spending it.

Three months went by. Her new doctors would not proceed with surgery, and suggested she have more chemotherapy. Before going ahead, but after incurring heavy debt, Behnaz returned to her original oncologist who ordered radiotherapy. Traveling across the city by bus for two hours each way while ill, for a 10-minute radiotherapy session daily is more than many of us could imagine possible. Behnaz made it to many of the appointments, but in the end, she abandoned the radiotherapy for another source of support and hope for a promised cure. Behnaz's strong desire to live drove her in different directions to explore all options.

Five months went by. The center was closed for a month in the summer. The next month we were only open one day per week. In the fall, when we had a full complement of volunteers again, I asked our translator to please call to check on Behnaz. Her number was still active, but calls did not always go through. Finally, we made contact. When I saw her enter the garden gate, I was both overjoyed and crushed. I ushered her into my office and had only the translator and one other nurse stay with me. Behnaz was weak and frail, and I recognized the smell of death. From many years as a hospice nurse, I knew it too well. This was more than infection; it was decay. I hugged Behnaz, and both of us cried. I asked if I could see her wound, and care for her. It was painful to see her so weak. She had never had surgery, and her body showed the evidence. We washed her, gave her bandage supplies for use at home and prayed with her. We gave her a hot meal as well as nonperishable food to take home. We gave her a new top as her clothes were soiled with the same smell. Behnaz was dying.

It became a priority for me to see Behnaz in her home and talk with her about her thoughts for her next steps. Along with another volunteer who spoke Dari, we headed out to an address that Behnaz had provided by phone. Her neighborhood was two hours west by public transportation. We had a bag of groceries and some more medical supplies for her to continue to clean her decaying flesh. Once in the neighborhood we wandered, searching for the address. Suddenly Leyla burst out of an apartment building door, ran to the middle of the street, and wrapped her arms around me in a tight hug! Her embrace is imprinted on my memory. Excitedly she directed us to their apartment. Behnaz was frail, but her smile was bright. She had used all of her energy that morning to cook us a costly meal. We sat on the living room floor and feasted together.

That would be our last shared meal, and our last visit. Behnaz had come to understand that the disease was winning. She was in pain. She had debt. And she had a beautiful daughter. The internal call home became stronger than the call to a hoped-for but unattainable future. Behnaz never spoke to me about her decision to return to Afghanistan. The news came to me by a voice message on WhatsApp. Behnaz had often left voice messages, so that was not surprising. But I was caught off guard when I heard her voice and her message saying that she was in Kabul. The news hit me hard. I cried. I would not see her again. My role of health advocate in her fight against cancer was over. For Behnaz I could take comfort that she was now home with some of her family to care for her in her dying days. But for Leyla, I felt deep loss and fear. What would her future be?

Within a few weeks my messages went unanswered. The message line fell silent.

In my grief, and in the silence, I found comfort in the prayer of Lilias Trotter, an artist and missionary who served in North Africa. Her repeated threefold prayer was, "That doors might be opened; that hearts might be opened; and that the heavens might be opened" (Miriam Huffman Rockness, Passion for the Impossible). God knows each story and cares far more than I do. This was not a closed door to him. He can still call her to himself; he can reveal himself to her. Like the leper in Luke's Gospel who said, "Lord, if you will, you can," I prayed that her heart would be opened – and that heaven would open to her as well.

Joan had not visited our office for six years. We had served her during two pregnancies; then she had seemed to disappear. When she arrived at the center, Joan was clearly drained. Her children were not with her. One was in school, and one was with a friend. Joan had traveled for almost two hours on public transit to get to us. She needed help. Her husband was sick in the hospital and not responding well. She reported that doctors had ignored a longstanding cough that he complained of. They told him on multiple occasions that it must be a lingering effect of Covid-19.

As she shared more information, tears came to her eyes. I moved from behind my desk and came to sit beside her. I put my arm around her shoulder to comfort her as I listened. Her body began to shake with sobs. She was afraid. She did not know what was wrong. "He has not seemed right in the head, and he does not answer me," she told me. Joan had been bearing this burden alone. She recalled how one day he was unresponsive and she called an ambulance to bring him to the hospital. The doctors ran tests and told her that he had TB in his head. "What is that?" asked Joan. "What does it mean?" Without any documentation of his diagnosis, I did not want to overwhelm her. I had just enough information to say that it was a very good thing that he was in the hospital. We gave Joan financial help and told her we would give more. We encouraged her to return with documents. We prayed together and she was very appreciative of the support.

A few weeks went by, and Joan did not return. I called, and she shared that her husband had died. I expressed my deep grief and told her to come whenever it worked for her. A couple of people went out to her home with gifts for the children, food for the family, and time to just sit and grieve with Joan.

Joan had lost the love of her life, her partner and provider. Now the hospital refused to release his body to Joan until the bill could be paid in full. The family in Nigeria sent money to help; other friends took on debt to assist her. An African pastor went to the hospital and stayed until they gave the body over for burial.

Joan returned each month for a few months so that we could talk and pray and assist her with basic needs for herself and the children. Her family in Nigeria wanted the two children to be sent to them, but they wanted Joan to stay in Turkey and work and send money. But the children needed their mother, and she desperately needed them. Her grief was raw. Turkey was not home, but it was all that the children had known together, and it was the only place they had memories of their father. In this season they needed each other, and our office had become a place where they could find sanctuary and help.

Death humbles us. It reminds us to "number our days, that we may gain a heart of wisdom." The stories of Gaspard, Behnaz, and Joan are reminders of the limits of our best efforts. We can work, we can serve, we can show compassion and love, but the end of the story is beyond our control. Where can we turn in the face of grief and silence?

To give them a beautiful headdress instead of ashes, the oil of gladness instead of mourning, the garment of praise instead of a faint spirit.

Isaiah 61:3

I woke one morning in Massachusetts to two important messages. The first was an encouraging email with news of a generous gift to our refugee center. The donation would contribute to the cost of medical care for Blessing, a baby born with a serious heart defect requiring major cardiac surgery. As we've seen, to be a refugee or migrant is difficult under the best of circumstances; but when a refugee mom gives birth to a child with a life-threatening condition, her situation becomes overwhelming. The cost of this kind of medical care is well beyond our center's resources. Together with other partner agencies, we set out to raise money for the costly surgery. I shared the story of Blessing with some friends as one example of the overwhelming situations that we see. Their generous response was a great blessing, and I was deeply grateful for that first message.

After reading the email, I opened my text messages. One of our partners in Istanbul wrote to let me know that Blessing had died. I didn't know any details. I was far removed from the situation. One moment I was rejoicing to learn that we had money to contribute toward saving a baby's life; the next moment I was grieving. Blessing was gone.

We are all familiar with this tension of joy and sorrow colliding. Death is not a stranger, and grief is a constant presence in our groaning world; but joy and beauty are also everywhere. And we know, by faith, that beauty and joy will win.

People often ask me, "How do you handle the burdens of helping refugees in such difficult circumstances?" It is a good question. Increasingly, I am learning that I need to soak in beauty while engaging in the burdens of brokenness. Beauty is a restorative gift from God. The beauty of creation is all around us. Psalm 19 tells us that creation speaks aloud the goodness of God and the glory of God. Driving through green mountains and forests, sitting beside the deep blue waters of a lake, walking along the shores of the vast ocean, looking up at cloud formations or brilliance of the stars, we should be overwhelmed by majestic beauty. Beauty is God's gift to us, it speaks to the soul, and it directs our hearts towards our Creator.

God surrounds us with beauty, and he made us creative. Being made in the image of God, we are creative because God is. When we create, we experience the joy of beauty. To craft a sentence and express yourself just right; to dance, sew, paint, sing, compose, sculpt, build, draw, record, photograph, play an instrument; to engage in any creative venture – these are ways to absorb beauty. We can make an active choice to push back at brokenness and pain, to overwrite it; God is making all things new, and one day all the sad things will become untrue.

God made each of us in his image. We are creative and we can enjoy both the image and the creative efforts in the people around us. There is no shortage of variety in our world. We are all so different. Do you or I look with curiosity and notice these differences as the hand of our creative God?

Each woman who comes to the center is marked with a distinctive beauty. Even as I need to seek beauty in active ways as I hear and know the brokenness and trauma around me, I also take joy in encouraging the women to do the same. Asking them to look up at the sky, the trees, the clouds is a simple but possible way to encourage their seeking of beauty.

Samina is young, beautiful, tall, the mother of a two-year-old girl. She entered our small, one-room office looking weary and weighted. We had talked the month before, when she first visited our program. Her husband had been deported. All of their documents were with him. She is alone in Istanbul, vulnerable, without a clear path forward.

Samina sat down next to my desk, and we talked together for a few minutes to catch up. No, she had not heard from her husband. No, she had no other family connections in Istanbul. Yes, the family she is living with will continue to allow her and her daughter to use one room in their apartment. The two families only met a few months ago soon after Samina and her husband arrived. They have no resources to offer her other than the one room to spare. They are counting on her continuing to share the rent.

Samina found work washing dishes. Her employer fired her after two days because she brought her daughter. He refused to pay her for the work she did.

As we talked, Samina shared that her back had been hurting. I asked her to show me where, and started to rub it. When I touched her, tears fell down her cheeks. This beautiful twenty-two-year-old carried so much weight. "When did someone last care for her and hold her?" I wondered. I hugged her, and her daughter looked on with concern. She wanted to be part of the hugging too.

Our encounter was brief, but it lingered with me. The embrace with Samina was a gift from God to me, and it seemed to be equally significant to her. Time and touch had been two ways to care for Samina. Samina's posture on leaving the garden gave indication of a lighter spirit. She spent some time at the craft table working with beads to make a bracelet. Volunteers played with her daughter. Samina left with a food package in hand and an appointment to return in a month.

Refugees and migrants share stories of poverty, injustice, and illness with us each day. Many of these, like Samina's story, are heartbreaking. They can leave me and our volunteers drained of joy. It is part of the role of coordinator to share stories at the monthly board meetings. After one meeting, a board member saw that I was burdened. She challenged me to look for moments of joy, and to report these back to the board at the next meeting. It was a good exercise. I appreciated her care; it had encouraged me to look with new eyes. What would I report back that joy looked like?

A woman came to us with a four-day-old baby. She carried the bundled baby together with a burden of hopelessness and despair. The bills were far beyond the family's ability to handle. She pleaded with us for help with the cost of birthing this new life. We could have just focused on the need. But then we would have missed what was most important at that moment. Here in our office was a beautiful, new life, a precious gift of God. I stood up, stepped away from the desk, and held the baby, rejoicing in the miracle of new life. Thanks be to God for new babies! I engaged in seeing and speaking the beauty of life and encouraged the mother to see as well.

Another young woman had overwhelming physical needs. She required surgery, but the cost would be prohibitive. Her Turkish physician donated his time and talents for her surgery, reducing her bill from 85,000 TL to 30,000 TL. She was struggling over where the remaining 30,000 TL would come from. I encouraged her to pause with me and be amazed at the generosity of the surgeon. "This is not a normal everyday occurrence. This is a huge gift, and it is for you!"

Midway through a cold and difficult day, I walked to the back of the garden to peek inside the shelter. The children were warm and happy as they sat around tables playing games and doing crafts. A heated shelter for the children and creative volunteers to run a children's program are causes for joy!

A woman came to us following what sounded like poor care from a back-alley clinic. We were able to send her to the hospital and provide her with good care. Her smile and appreciation were a moment of joy!

Jesus came to our office! The baby boy, wrapped up in too many layers, was across the desk from me. His mom had come to us for help with the cost of his birth. "What is his name?" I asked. "Isa," she told me. I smiled. "Do you know İsa Mesih?" I asked. She smiled back. "Yes, that is who he is named after." Jesus was not the only surprise guest that day! The next two newborns in the office were Abraham and Joseph. I am thankful for the precious joy of new life and shared spiritual heritage with our Muslim friends.

The reality is that Jesus comes to our office every day. He shows his love through the hands and feet of those serving the vulnerable in his name and for his glory. I was thankful that the board member helped me in my struggle to push against the brokenness, pain, and injustice and to seek and speak beauty. I was able to share with the board and with others that "Jesus comes to our office."

Epilogue

... being born in the likeness of men. And being found in human form, he humbled himself by becoming obedient to the point of death, even death on a cross.

Philippians 2:7-8

Those who have walked into our garden during the last three decades bear the scars of cruelty, conflict, and injustice. Our volunteers have cared for those fleeing from the Iraq war, from the oppession of the Iranian regime, from the Bosnian genocide, from the occupation of Palestine, from the Syrian civil war, the war in Ukraine, and from the brutality of the Taliban. We have welcomed those displaced by poverty and conflict in Africa; we have cried with victims of slavery; we have cared for those suffering from AIDS and losing family members to Ebola. Members of our network have visited those unjustly imprisoned, have fed the hungry, have offered winter coats to children without them. We have seen firsthand the cruel denial of personhood to those who lack documents, and the ravages of disease on those most vulnerable.

People who have endured cruelty, injustice, violence, and war are not an abstraction. They have names and faces. For those of us who have worked side by side in Istanbul, they are mothers like Hanife, left alone with small children and no papers; Jamila, enduring widowhood and poverty; and Behnaz, whose fierce determination was ultimately defeated by cancer. They are young men like Gaspard, stranded between nations, and Shahram, whose conscience cost him his safety. They are children like little Ali, born too soon into a fragile world, and Yusuf, whose arm hangs limp from a preventable injury.

Where is God in their stories?

In Lament for a Son, Nicholas Wolterstorff wrestles with suffering, pain, and death following the death of his son Eric in a mountaineering accident:

> It is said of God that no one can behold his face and live. I always thought this meant that no one could see his splendor and live. A friend said that perhaps it meant that no one could see his sorrow and live. Or perhaps his sorrow is splendor.
>
> And great mystery: to redeem our brokenness and lovelessness the God who suffers with us did not strike some mighty blow of power but sent his beloved son to suffer like us, through his suffering to redeem us from suffering and evil.

Instead of explaining our suffering, God shares it.

The large front wall of the Church of the Resurrection in Anafora is dominated by an icon of the resurrected, ascended, and glorified Christ. It is one of the few icons that feels grand, and even glorious. The colors are pure white, soft blue, and majestic gold. But look closely. In Christ's halo is the image of a cross. Of course, the Cross. The symbol of his suffering is the symbol of his costly love and victory.

From the start of his life, Jesus was no stranger to suffering. As a child, he had to escape to Egypt with his parents, saving their lives from the murderous Herod. He was a refugee. Once he began his earthly ministry of teaching, Jesus was surrounded by critics. It was not long before they were plotting to kill him. When he did heal and perform miracles, Jesus was sought after by so many that he had to be on the move and became weary. He had to go out into desolate places to get any rest. Jesus had no place to call home for the three years that he was teaching. "The Son of Man has nowhere to lay his head," he said of himself. He entered our world as God's promised Savior. But he saved by suffering in the places and ways we suffer, by truly being with us. He became the object of human cruelty, injustice, mockery, hatred, and torture.

My eyes move back from the image of the glorified Christ at the front of the church to the side wall and the icon with which we started. Here too Christ appears glorified, as judge at the end of the age. But the face of the judge is also the face of the prisoner, the face of the hungry, the face of the thirsty, the face of the naked, the face of the sick. This is not just a metaphor, a clever parable calculated to inspire us to service. It portrays the power and mystery of the Incarnation. United with us in flesh, God in Christ hungered, thirsted, suffered, died.

As I shared with so many women, God saw Hagar in her despair. He sees us. It is not a seeing from a distance. It is a seeing that responds and makes his seeing known. God appeared to Hagar. He entered her story and promised to provide for her. He revealed himself to Hagar as the God who sees and is seen. We need to see God and to see that God sees us. God's seeing and providing go together. Because God took on flesh in the person of Christ, he knows; he feels; he understands; he is Immanuel, God with us.

Who are the hungry, thirsty, alien, imprisoned, and sick in your world today? In this era of history the Church has a unique opportunity to distinguish itself from the callousness of our cultures and the cruelty of our governments. All over the world, walls are being built to keep out the alien, the stranger, the refugee, the victim of injustice. God asks us to do the opposite, because he tore down walls. Ask God to give you eyes to see Christ in your neighbor. At the start of this book, I set out to tell stories that might stimulate each of us in our care of the stranger in our midst. The partnership of the churches of Istanbul over more than 30 years is a humble, but powerful example. In some ways it is unique. In other ways it is happening all over the world. What is happening in your corner of the world? How can you be involved?

And in the end, because Jesus, who suffered, is Lord and Judge, joy, beauty, and justice will prevail.

To God be the Glory

www.ingramcontent.com/pod-product-compliance
Lightning Source LLC
LaVergne TN
LVHW010703110826
845149LV00014B/3216

* 9 7 8 0 9 9 8 2 2 3 3 8 4 *